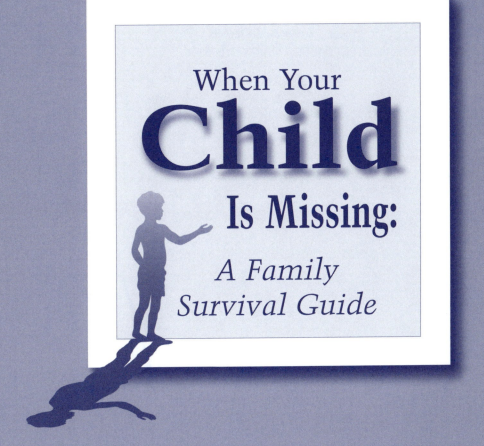

When Your Child Is Missing:
A Family Survival Guide

J. Robert Flores, Administrator
Office of Juvenile Justice and Delinquency Prevention
Office of Justice Programs
U.S. Department of Justice

NCJ 204958

Third Edition
May 2004

U.S. Department of Justice
Office of Justice Programs
Office of Juvenile Justice and Delinquency Prevention
810 Seventh Street NW.
Washington, DC 20531

John Ashcroft
Attorney General

Deborah J. Daniels
Assistant Attorney General

J. Robert Flores
Administrator

This document was prepared by Fox Valley Technical College under cooperative agreement number 98–MC–CX–K010 from the Office of Juvenile Justice and Delinquency Prevention, U.S. Department of Justice. This edition is updated from the second printing.

The Office of Juvenile Justice and Delinquency Prevention is a component of the Office of Justice Programs, which also includes the Bureau of Justice Assistance, the Bureau of Justice Statistics, the National Institute of Justice, and the Office for Victims of Crime.

I remember standing in the middle of the chaos thinking, I wish I had a book to tell me what to do.

—Colleen Nick

Message from Attorney General John Ashcroft on Missing Children's Day:

When a child is taken, a family is devastated. When a child disappears, the absence and pain ripples throughout the entire community, and even the country. When children are exploited or mistreated, and that natural spark in their eyes is diminished, our world is diminished.

Every day, families and law enforcement work hard to protect our children. No parent wants to experience the anguish of a missing child, but if that dreaded moment should occur, this guide will be a valuable resource for family members.

When Your Child is Missing: A Family Survival Guide was written by parents and family members whose children were abducted, and tragically murdered, or are still missing. It provides helpful and practical tips for families about what to do when their child is missing and how to best help law enforcement in the search and recovery of their child.

All Americans, however, play a vital role in protecting our children. A national awareness about missing children's issues means more homecomings for those that are lost. Together we can, and we must, work to ensure the safety of our children.

Sincerely,

John Ashcroft

A Message from Assistant Attorney General Deborah J. Daniels

Nearly 800,000 children are reported missing each year, for a variety of reasons: some children run away, others may become lost or injured, and still others are abducted.

Most child abductions-- more than 200,000 annually --are committed by family members, who are seeking to interfere with a parent's custodial rights. Of the non-family abductions, totaling 58,200 annually in the United States, nearly all (98%) of these children are returned to their families safely. Only a small percentage are those every parent most dreads: those we call "stereotypical kidnappings," in which the child is kept overnight, held for ransom, or killed. However, in these cases in particular, the first few hours after the abduction are critical. This *Guide* provides parents with important tools to assist them in the safe return of their children.

I am pleased that the publication of this updated edition of *When Your Child Is Missing: A Family Survival Guide* coincides with Missing Children's Day. The U.S. Justice Department, through its Office of Justice Programs, is honored to support this valuable effort to help ensure the safety of the nation's children.

Deborah J. Daniels
Assistant Attorney General

Foreword

In an instant, a peaceful day can become a nightmare when a child is discovered missing. We have witnessed tragic abductions of children of all ages across America—in rural byways and major cities. We have also been heartened by the joyful reunions of children safely returned to their parents.

Children may be missing from home for a variety of reasons. They may run away after a heated argument with their parents or be lured away by an online predator in an Internet chatroom. They may be taken by a noncustodial parent to another country—perhaps to strike back at an ex-spouse—or abducted by someone the child does not know.

Whatever the reason a child is missing, parents' lives are turned upside down, and minutes race into hours as they frantically seek their child's return to the safety of home. We know that time is of the essence in terms of finding a child. What should parents do if their child is missing? To whom can they turn? What help can they expect?

When Your Child Is Missing: A Family Survival Guide was written as a labor of love and a vision of hope by parents who have experienced firsthand the trauma of a missing child. It has been updated to provide parents the most current information available and provides helpful insights into what families should do—and what they can expect—when a child is missing. Above all, it offers encouragement and support at a time when they are needed most.

I pray that you will never experience the trauma of a missing child and that every child will be kept safe from harm and danger. Should your child become missing, however, I hope that this *Guide* gives you the knowledge to face this terrible challenge with strength and determination.

J. Robert Flores
Administrator
Office of Juvenile Justice and Delinquency Prevention

Acknowledgments

The Office of Juvenile Justice and Delinquency Prevention (OJJDP) is grateful to all of the people who gave their time, energy, and talent to developing this *Guide,* especially the following parents who know firsthand the pain, suffering, and hope of families with missing children:

> **Heather Cox and Marion Boburka, mother and grandmother, respectively, of Shelby Cox, who was found murdered on November 18, 1995.**

> **Colleen Nick, mother of Morgan Nick, who has been missing since June 9, 1995.**

> **Claudine and Don Ryce, parents of Jimmy Ryce, who was found murdered on December 9, 1995.**

> **Patrick Sessions, father of Tiffany Sessions, who has been missing since February 9, 1989.**

> **Patty Wetterling, mother of Jacob Wetterling, who has been missing since October 22, 1989.**

This group of parents created this *Guide* as a labor of love and as a message of hope and encouragement for families whose children are still missing. Their courage and strength are greatly admired.

OJJDP also thanks the many professionals who have given their time and effort to find children who are missing, who have worked to prevent children from being abducted, and who have put together this *Guide* for families facing this crisis. This includes Helen Connelly, James P. Finley, and Joellen Talbot of Fox Valley Technical College. The final editing and production of this *Guide* were performed by the Juvenile Justice Clearinghouse. OJJDP acknowledges C. Denise Collins and Annie Pardo for graphic support with this 2004 update and Irene Cooperman and Beverly Sullivan for editorial support. OJJDP also acknowledges and thanks the many individuals who painstakingly reviewed the *Guide* to make sure that it provides parents with the information they so desperately need during these crises. Special thanks also go to Ron Laney, Director of OJJDP's Child Protection Division. His concern for and commitment to missing children and their parents inspired the creation of this *Guide.*

This *Guide* is dedicated to all the children who are separated from their families. Our hope is that you always know that the search will continue until you are found.

Table of Contents

Introduction

When your child is missing, your whole world seems to fall apart. You are bombarded by questions from friends, neighbors, the police, and the media and forced to make decisions that you never thought you would have to make. You feel desperate, confused, isolated. You may feel that you have nowhere to go for help or support.

Many parents who have faced similar crises have said that they wished they had a book to tell them where to turn when their child was missing. They felt that they were left on their own to figure out what to do. They longed for someone to give them direction or to tell them where to go for help and what needs to be done. They also wished they had known what to expect and how to respond.

This *Guide* was written by parents and family members who have experienced the disappearance of a child. It contains their combined advice concerning what you can expect when your child is missing, what you can do, and where you can go for help. It explains the role that various agencies and organizations play in the search for your missing child and discusses some of the important issues that you and your family need to consider. The first checklist, What You Should Do When Your Child Is First Missing, summarizes the most critical steps that parents should take when their child is first missing, including whom to call, what to do to preserve evidence, and where to turn for help.

The rest of the *Guide* is divided into seven chapters, each of which is structured to allow you to find the information you need quickly and easily. Each chapter explains both the short- and long-term issues and contains a checklist and chapter summary for later reference. Chapter 1, The Search, focuses on the search for your child and explains how you as a parent can best participate in the search.

Chapter 2, Law Enforcement, describes your relationship with law enforcement and offers tips that will help you work together effectively. Chapter 3, The Media, examines issues related to the media, including media packages, press conferences, and interviews. Chapter 4, Photo and Flier Distribution, offers suggestions for producing fliers about your child and for managing the photo and flier distribution process. Chapter 5, Volunteers, focuses on the many uses of volunteers—both trained and untrained—to help in the search and to provide for the needs of the family. Chapter 6, Rewards and Donations, discusses the use of rewards and the management of monetary donations. Chapter 7, Personal and Family Considerations, emphasizes the need to take care of yourself, your children, and members of your extended family. A list of recommended readings and a list of public and private resources appear at the back of the *Guide*.

It is important to note that there is no right or wrong way to respond to the disappearance of a child, nor is there a right or wrong way to feel. The path you follow must be right for you. What makes sense for you will be based on your needs, your experiences, and your circumstances. Our hope is that the *Guide* will help you to make informed decisions about what you do and how you go about it.

You may find that the information in this *Guide* is overwhelming right now. If so, ask family members, friends, or other support persons to read it for you. They can help you take the steps needed to help recover your missing child.

Finally, as hard as it may seem, try to remain hopeful. Remember that hope is more than a wish, helping you to clear this hurdle. Hope is essential to your survival.

Checklist: What You Should Do When Your Child Is First Missing

The first 48 hours following the disappearance of a child are the most critical in terms of finding and returning that child safely home—but they also can be the most troublesome and chaotic. Use this checklist during those first hours to help you do everything you can to increase the chances of recovering your child—but if more than 48 hours have passed since your child disappeared, you should still try to tend to these items as quickly as possible. All of the action steps described here are covered in greater detail later in the Guide to help you gain a better understanding of what you should be doing and why.

The First 24 Hours

- [ ] **Immediately** report your child as missing to your local law enforcement agency. Ask investigators to enter your child into the National Crime Information Center (NCIC) Missing Persons File. There is no waiting period for entry into NCIC.

- [ ] **Request** that law enforcement put out a Be On the Look Out (BOLO) bulletin. Ask them about involving the Federal Bureau of Investigation (FBI) in the search for your child.

- [ ] **Ask** your law enforcement agency about the AMBER Alert Plan (America's Missing: Broadcast Emergency Response). Through AMBER Alert, law enforcement agencies and broadcasters activate an urgent bulletin in the most serious child abduction cases (see page 4 for more information on the AMBER Alert Plan).

- [ ] **Limit** access to your home until law enforcement arrives and has collected possible evidence. Do not touch or remove anything from your child's room or from your home. Remember that clothing, sheets, personal items, computers, and even trash may hold clues to the whereabouts of your child. The checklist in chapter 1 (Gathering Evidence in the First 48 Hours) contains detailed information about securing your child's room and preserving evidence.

- [ ] **Ask** for the name and telephone number of the law enforcement investigator assigned to your case, and keep this information in a safe and convenient place.

- [ ] **Give** law enforcement investigators all the facts and circumstances related to the disappearance of your child, including what efforts have already been made to search for your child.

- [ ] **Write** a detailed description of the clothing worn by your child and the personal items he or she had at the time of the disappearance. Include in your description any personal identification marks, such as birthmarks, scars, tattoos, or mannerisms, that may help in finding your child. If possible, find a picture of your child that shows these identification marks and give it to law enforcement. See the chapter 1 checklist (Gathering Evidence in the First 48 Hours) for more details.

- [ ] **Make** a list of friends, acquaintances, and anyone else who might have information or clues about your child's whereabouts. Include telephone numbers and addresses, if possible. Tell your law enforcement investigator about anyone who moved in or out of the neighborhood within the past year, anyone whose interest in or involvement with the family changed in recent months, and anyone who appeared to be overly interested in your child.

- [ ] **Find** recent photographs of your child in both black and white and color. Make copies of these pictures for your law enforcement agency, the media, your state missing children's clearinghouse, the National Center for Missing & Exploited Children® (NCMEC), and other nonprofit organizations. Chapter 4 (Photo and Flier Distribution) contains suggestions on how to produce and distribute fliers and posters.

- [ ] **Call** NCMEC at 800–THE–LOST® (800–843–5678) to ask for help. Also, ask for the telephone numbers of other nonprofit organizations that might be able to help.

- [ ] **Look** in the Additional Resources section at the end of this *Guide* to find the telephone number of your state missing children's clearinghouse. Then, call your clearinghouse to find out what resources and services it can provide in the search for your child.

- **Ask** your law enforcement agency to organize a search for your child. Ask them about using tracking or trailing dogs (preferably bloodhounds) in the search effort. Read chapters 1 (The Search) and 5 (Volunteers) as you prepare for the search.

- **Ask** your law enforcement agency for help in contacting the media. Chapter 3 (The Media) contains advice on working with the media.

- **Designate** one person to answer your telephone. Keep a notebook or pad of paper by the telephone so this person can jot down names, telephone numbers, dates and times of calls, and other information relating to each call.

- **Keep** a notebook or pad of paper with you at all times to write down your thoughts or questions and record important information, such as names, dates, or telephone numbers.

- **Take** good care of yourself and your family because your child needs you to be strong. As hard as it may be, force yourself to get rest, eat nourishing food, and talk to someone about your tumultuous feelings. When you can, read chapter 7 (Personal and Family Considerations).

The Second 24 Hours

- **Talk** with your law enforcement investigator about the steps that are being taken to find your child. If your law enforcement investigator does not have a copy of *Missing and Abducted Children: A Law Enforcement Guide to Case Investigation and Program Management,* suggest that he or she call NCMEC at 800–THE–LOST® (800–843–5678) to obtain one. Also, your law enforcement investigator can contact the Crimes Against Children Coordinator in the local FBI Field Office to obtain a copy of the FBI's *Child Abduction Response Plan.*

- **Expand** your list of friends, acquaintances, extended family members, yard workers, delivery persons, and anyone who may have seen your child during or following the abduction.

- **Look** at personal calendars, community events calendars, and newspapers to see if there are any clues as to who was in the vicinity and might be the abductor or a possible witness. Give this information to law enforcement.

- **Expect** that you will be asked to take a polygraph test, which is standard procedure. If you have not done so yet, read chapter 1 (The Search).

- **Ask** your law enforcement agency to request that NCMEC issue a broadcast fax to law enforcement agencies around the country. If you have not already read chapter 4 (Photo and Flier Distribution), try to read it now.

- **Work** with your law enforcement agency to schedule press releases and media events. If necessary, ask someone close to you to serve as your media spokesperson. Chapter 3 (The Media) provides tips on working with the media.

- **Talk** to your law enforcement agency about the use of a reward. When you can, read chapter 6 (Rewards and Donations).

- **Report** all extortion attempts to law enforcement.

- **Have** a second telephone line installed with call forwarding. Get caller ID and call waiting. Ask law enforcement to install a trap-and-trace feature on your phone. Get a cellular phone or pager so you can be reached when you are away from home.

- **Take** care of yourself. Don't be afraid to ask others to take care of your physical and emotional needs and those of your family. Read chapter 7 (Personal and Family Considerations) for specific suggestions.

- **Make** a list of things that volunteers can do for you and your family. See chapter 5 (Volunteers) for ideas.

- **Call** your child's doctor and dentist and ask for copies of medical records and x rays. Give them to law enforcement.

- **Talk** to your law enforcement agency about creating a Web site to capture information on leads. Designate a screened and trusted volunteer to manage the Web site.

The AMBER Alert Plan

What Is the AMBER Alert Plan?

The AMBER Alert Plan is a tool that law enforcement agencies can use to safely recover abducted children. It should be one component of the law enforcement agency's broader child recovery plan.

The AMBER Alert Plan is a voluntary partnership among law enforcement agencies, media outlets, and transportation agencies. This partnership focuses on the recovery of abducted children by disseminating timely and accurate information about the child, the suspected abductor, and the vehicle used in the commission of the crime. Through AMBER Alert, law enforcement agencies and broadcasters activate an urgent news bulletin in the most serious child abduction cases. Broadcasters use the Emergency Alert System (EAS), formerly called the Emergency Broadcast System, to air a description of the missing child and suspected abductor. Under appropriate circumstances, transportation authorities can use changeable message signs (CMS) to communicate important AMBER Alert information to motorists.

How Does the AMBER Alert Plan Work?

Once law enforcement is notified about an abducted child, it first determines if the case meets the AMBER Alert Plan's criteria for triggering an alert. The U.S. Department of Justice (DOJ) suggests that the following criteria be met before an alert is activated:

- Law enforcement believes an abduction has occurred.

- The child is 17 years old or younger.

- Law enforcement believes the child is in imminent danger of serious bodily harm or death.

- Sufficient descriptive information about the victim and the abduction exists to believe that an immediate AMBER Alert broadcast will help.

- The child's name and other critical information, including the fact that the case is considered a child abduction, have been entered into the NCIC system.

If these criteria are met, alert information is put together and faxed to media outlets designated as primary stations under EAS, which in turn send the same information to area radio, television, and cable systems where it is broadcast to millions of listeners. Radio stations interrupt programming to announce the alert and television and cable stations run a "crawl" on the screen with a picture of the missing child. CMS can also be used to display information to motorists.

For more information about the AMBER Alert Plan, visit DOJ's Web site at www.ojp.usdoj.gov/amberalert.

Is an AMBER Alert Issued for Every Missing Child?

AMBER Alerts are issued by a law enforcement agency in cooperation with the media if the circumstances surrounding the child's disappearance meet local or state AMBER Alert criteria. If the circumstances do not meet the criteria, remember that the media can still be called on to help in the recovery of your child. See chapter 3 (The Media).

> **I**f we could have gotten the word out immediately when Morgan disappeared, I'm certain she would be home with me today. With the AMBER Alert Plan . . . time is now on the side of every parent and child.
>
> —Colleen Nick

CHAPTER 1

The Search

Not knowing where your child is or if he or she is okay is the hardest thing in the world to handle.

—Colleen Nick

When a child is reported missing, emotions become raw, which can hinder the ability of parents to make rational decisions. Yet, the actions of parents and of law enforcement in the first 48 hours are critical to the safe recovery of a missing child. Knowing what you can do, what others can do, and where to go for help will not only expedite the search and recovery of your child, it also will help to ease the emotional and financial burden of the search. This chapter examines your role and the role of others in the immediate search for your missing child and discusses what steps should be taken in the event that your child does not return within the first few days.

Your Role in the Search: The First 48 Hours

In the initial stage of the search, devote your time to providing information to and answering questions from investigators. Once you discover that your child is missing, you will desperately want to help with the search. You may, in fact, wonder how you possibly can stand by and let others look for your child. But the reality is that in most instances, the best use of your energy is not on the physical search itself. Rather, you need to provide information to and answer questions from

investigators and to be at home in the event your child calls. The checklist Gathering Evidence in the First 48 Hours identifies the most crucial pieces of background information and evidence that law enforcement will need in the search for your child.

The Role of Law Enforcement in the Search

When a child has disappeared, most of the initial searching of the area where the child is believed to have been last will be coordinated by law enforcement—either federal, state, or local, depending on the circumstances of the disappearance. Law enforcement needs to direct the search effort in order to make sure that the search is performed properly and that the evidence located during the search—and at the crime scene—is properly protected and preserved.

Usually, law enforcement agencies can quickly obtain the necessary equipment and mobilize additional personnel by bringing in outside forces. Because time is a critical factor in the search and recovery effort, equipment and staff should be requested at

I remember sitting around our kitchen table on the first night our son was taken when the investigators asked me, "Is there anybody who liked Jacob too much? Who gave him special attention or presents? Who wanted to take him places?" I never dreamed that a nice person could have taken our son or that the most common lure is attention and affection.

—Patty Wetterling

the beginning of the process. Your local agency may request that tracking or trailing dogs, infrared devices that locate heat given off from the body, or helicopters be delivered to the scene and may request help from the Border Patrol, the Coast Guard, the National Guard, other military personnel, or correctional institution staff. Many of these groups are already trained in search procedures, and their established chain of command makes the search effort more likely to be thorough, comprehensive, and efficient. In addition, the FBI maintains Field Offices that have Evidence Response Teams that could be of assistance in cases of missing or abducted children. Your local law enforcement agency may issue an AMBER Alert. Do not hesitate to ask the agency about the steps it will take to safely locate and return your child.

In many communities, law enforcement agencies have an established child recovery plan, similar to an emergency relief or disaster plan, to guide their search and recovery efforts. Ask your law enforcement agency about its plan. Make sure the agency has a copy of *Missing and Abducted Children: A Law Enforcement Guide to Case Investigation and Program Management* (published by NCMEC), which provides step-by-step instructions on how to respond to and investigate missing children cases and details procedures for conducting and managing the search. Also, make sure that your law enforcement agency has a copy of the *Child Abduction Response Plan* (published by the FBI and available from

local Crimes Against Children Coordinators in FBI Field Offices), which emphasizes the techniques that are essential in conducting abduction investigations.

Typically, your law enforcement agency will designate one or two persons to coordinate and manage the search. Ask for the name and telephone number of your law enforcement coordinator as soon as possible. Keep this information where you can find it in a safe, convenient place. Keep the lines of communication open between you and your search coordinator. Don't be afraid to ask questions, make suggestions, or air differences of opinion.

Find out what types of searches are planned. Searches can be conducted in several ways:

■ A crime scene search of the areas where your child was last seen.

■ A door-to-door search.

■ A grid search.

■ A land, sea, or air search.

■ A roadblock search, which may involve stopping cars at the same time of day at the location where your child was last seen. Because people are creatures of habit and tend to take the same route each day, roadblock searches sometimes produce witnesses who saw your child, who observed someone hanging around the area, or who remember an out-of-place vehicle.

Telephone Tips

☎ If you do not already have one, buy a cellular phone or pager so you can be reached when you are away from home.

☎ Ask law enforcement to install a trap and trace on your phone.

☎ Install a phone with the ability to tape calls.

☎ Ask your telephone company to install caller ID on your telephone line.

☎ Keep a phone log, a pad of paper, or a spiral notebook next to the phone to record the date and time of phone calls, the name of the caller, and other information.

Ask your search coordinator what types of searches are being conducted, and make sure you feel comfortable that the search effort is adequate.

Records documenting which areas were searched, who was present, and what was found will be kept. Law enforcement will maintain a record showing what areas have been searched and by whom. A second search of critical areas for information and clues might be advisable because something may have been overlooked during the initial search.

Tracking or trailing dogs, preferably bloodhounds, should be brought immediately to the scene where your child was last seen. The fresher the trail, the more likely the dogs will be able to find your child. Bloodhounds are your best bet because they have 60 times the tracking power of German shepherds, can discriminate among scents, and can follow your child's scent in the air and on the ground. This means that they may be able to pick up your child's scent even if he or she was carried in someone's arms or in a vehicle.

The Role of Volunteers in the Search

If volunteers are used in the search, your law enforcement agency should still be responsible for managing the overall search effort. The extent to which volunteers are used in the search will depend on whether additional personnel—beyond the military—are needed. A volunteer search coordinator may be needed to organize the volunteer search effort.

Try to recruit established organizations, agencies, or groups—rather than individual volunteers—in the search. The use of affiliated groups makes it possible to quickly gather and organize a large number of volunteers. It also provides an inner chain of command, which makes communication and training easier, and provides an internal screening mechanism.

When volunteers are used, request that the volunteer staging area be located away from your home. There will be enough traffic, chaos, and confusion at your home without the added burden of volunteer search teams.

All volunteer searchers should be required to sign in each time they participate in a search activity. The sign-in procedure can be as simple as asking the volunteer searchers to show their driver's licenses and to list in a log book their names, addresses, and organizational affiliations, such as the Boy Scouts, local labor union, place of business, or local post of the Veterans of Foreign Wars. Keep all records for future reference.

A more elaborate sign-in procedure involves videotaping the sign-in and search efforts. Although it is impossible to videotape every search from start to finish, videotapes that show the searchers, the sign-in process, and the search locations can provide valuable information about possible clues and suspects. Some situations that seem innocent initially, such as the repeated appearance of an overly concerned searcher, may not be as innocent as they appear.

Request that law enforcement run background checks for prior criminal activity on persons volunteering for the search. In previous cases, thieves, pedophiles, and even the missing child's abductor have been known to join in a search. Background checks can prevent misguided people from volunteering and sometimes can provide information that helps law enforcement conduct the search.

Have your volunteer coordinator talk with law enforcement to determine whether additional equipment or personnel are needed. Contact local businesses, missing children's organizations, NCMEC, your state missing children's clearinghouse, or other agencies to obtain the necessary supplies or tap into a network of people.

Further information about resources that can help with the search can be obtained by calling NCMEC. Established in 1984 as a private, nonprofit organization, NCMEC serves as a clearinghouse of information on missing and exploited children. It also provides technical assistance to both citizens and law enforcement agencies, distributes photographs and descriptions of missing children nationwide, and networks with nonprofit service providers and state clearinghouses on missing children. NCMEC can be contacted at its headquarters in Virginia or in one of its five branch offices in California, Florida, Missouri, New York, and South Carolina.

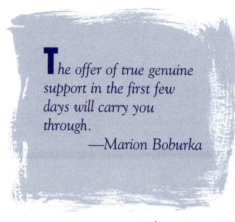

The offer of true genuine support in the first few days will carry you through.

—Marion Boburka

you have new, important information, make sure that you give it to law enforcement as soon as possible. Ask your law enforcement agency about using the services of Team Adam to assist with the ongoing investigation (Team Adam is described on page 21).

Ask to see your child's case file periodically. You may recognize something meaningful that was overlooked or remember something significant that law enforcement was not aware of. Be aware that there may be pieces of information that law enforcement cannot— or does not want to—release to you because it may jeopardize or hinder the investigation. This is okay. Some states do not allow the release of police reports until a case is closed. Ask your search coordinator what information can be legally released to you or what you are allowed to see.

After the First 48 Hours: The Long-Term Search

When the search for a child becomes long term, not all parents can or will want to be actively involved in the search. It is okay if you choose not to be involved. But if you want to remain active in the long-term search effort, there are a number of things that you and other family members, friends, or volunteers can do to aid in the process.

Develop a plan and set a schedule with goals for continuing the search for your child. Work with law enforcement to figure out what role you and others can play in the long-term search. This *Guide* can help, especially chapters 3 (The Media) and 4 (Photo and Flier Distribution).

Schedule regular visits with your investigator. Set up a schedule for you and your investigator to review the status of the investigation and to give each other updates. However, if

Keep a spiral notebook with you to record your thoughts and review it periodically. When you reread your notebook or journal, you may find a passage that triggers a new idea or reminds you of something you had previously forgotten. Advise law enforcement about any new thoughts you have about the disappearance of your child.

Consider offering a reward for the safe return of your child. Chapter 6 contains specific information on the reward offer.

Find out what Crime Stoppers can do to help with the search. Crime Stoppers answers telephone calls 24 hours a day, knows how to take tip information, promises anonymity to callers, and maintains a good working relationship with law enforcement. If you like, ask to attend one of their meetings. If they agree, their telephone number may be a good choice for calls about a reward, because NCMEC will not provide reward information on its toll-free line.

Inquire about other programs that can be used for crime tips and rewards. Talk with your law enforcement agency and prosecutor's office to see if they know of other local, state, regional, or national programs that can be used to report crime tips or offer rewards.

Contact NCMEC, the state missing children's clearinghouses in the 50 states, and other missing children's organizations across the country. Ask for assistance with distribution of posters and fliers. Ask each agency what types of services it has available to assist with the search. Addresses and phone numbers for the missing children's clearinghouses in the 50 states, the District of Columbia, Canada, and Puerto Rico are listed in the Additional Resources section of this *Guide*. Some parents create a Web site to gather information on potential leads. Talk to your law enforcement agency about this and ask for its input. Use only screened and trusted volunteers to manage the Web site.

Keep community awareness of your plight at a high level. If your child has been missing for several years, ask NCMEC to develop an age-progressed picture, then place this picture next to the original picture on shirts, buttons, and posters. Chapter 4 contains sample fliers you can use as models for your own fliers. Also, if there is new information about your child—such as a sighting or an interesting lead—make sure that the public is kept informed. But before you disclose any information, be sure to consult with your law enforcement contact so the investigation is not compromised.

Keep the media interested and involved. Chapter 3 contains ideas for keeping the media interested in your story.

Make a list of things that others can do to help. As long as you have specific tasks for volunteers to perform, they won't go away.

Getting Help From Political Figures

The media often take special interest in publicizing cases in which political figures are involved. You can solicit help from school board members; city commissioners; your state Governor, senators, and representatives; and members of the U.S. House and Senate. You can also seek out those individuals who can get your child's poster displayed in the following public places:

- [ ] On buses, on subways, and at transfer points.
- [ ] In parks and other recreational facilities.
- [ ] At tollbooths and rest areas.
- [ ] In U.S. post offices.
- [ ] In state and federal buildings.[1]

Be wary, however, of attempts by well-meaning politicians to involve you in hastily written legislative proposals that could in the long run be detrimental to the plight of your child and others like him or her. Too often, legislative change comes about as a reaction to an incident, not as a well-planned, proactive response to a problem. Therefore, consider carefully the potential repercussions of any legislative proposal before you become involved.

---

[1] Authorized by Presidential Executive memorandum on January 19, 1996. This program requires federal agencies to receive and post missing children fliers in their buildings. This program is coordinated by NCMEC.

The Role of Private Detectives and Psychics in the Long-Term Search

Private Detectives

If the immediate search is not successful, you may be tempted to try almost anything. Some parents turn to private detectives to aid in the search.

Consider hiring a private detective or investigator *only* if you are convinced that he or she can do something better or different than what is being done by law enforcement. Be certain that you are not simply wasting money that could be spent more productively in another way. If you decide to use a private detective, the following tips can help:

- Always ask for and check references to find out if the investigator is legitimate.

- Be wary of people who say they can bring your child back immediately for a specific sum of money. If you run into this situation, report it to law enforcement.

- Make sure you are paying a reasonable rate. Insist that the investigator itemize expenses.

- Make sure the detective has experience working with law enforcement. Law enforcement must be notified immediately of any leads you receive from a private investigator.

- Inform your assigned law enforcement investigator about your decision to hire a private investigator. In most instances, this individual will need to talk to law enforcement before becoming involved in the case.

Psychics

Keep an open mind—*and a closed pocketbook*—when considering the use of a psychic. Most parents are desperate to try anything, but they need to understand that there are very few true psychics. Many are fraudulent or, at best, misguided individuals who want to help so much that they have self-induced visions. Hearing their sometimes negative dreams and visions can cause undue stress, a loss of hope, or an unfounded sense of hope. If you are considering turning to a psychic, remember the following tips:

- Ask someone close to the family to record any psychic leads because the information is usually distressing. Give all such leads to law enforcement.

- If any lead is highly specific, such as a particular address, insist that law enforcement check it out. Follow up with law enforcement to find out the value of the lead.

- Never allow a psychic to go into your child's room unattended or to take items without making arrangements for their return.

Regardless of whether some psychics have true visions, any purportedly psychic dream may be an actual observation by someone who is afraid to get involved. That is why even psychic leads need to be checked out whenever possible.

> I *was in tears as my husband kept sending our child's belongings to psychics. We still haven't gotten back his stuffed animals.*
> —Patty Wetterling

Overzealous Individuals

Be prepared to encounter a few people who are fanatical or obsessive in their behavior or in their desire to help. Keep in mind that some people may try to use your loss to gain attention for themselves. Protect yourself from people who might be delusional or who may prey on victims through scams or by offering false hopes and expectations. The key is to keep your focus and exercise caution.

Key Points

1. The actions of parents and of law enforcement in the first 48 hours are critical to the safe recovery of a missing child, but the rawness of emotion can seriously hinder the ability of parents to make rational decisions at this crucial time.

2. Your initial role in the search is to provide information to and answer questions from investigators and to be at home in the event your child calls.

3. Most of the initial searching of the area where the child is believed to have been last will be coordinated by law enforcement—either federal, state, or local, depending on the circumstances of the disappearance.

4. An important aspect of law enforcement's job is to preserve and protect any evidence gathered during the search.

5. Keep the name and telephone number of your law enforcement coordinator in a safe, convenient place. Keep the lines of communication open between you and your search coordinator by asking questions, making suggestions, and airing differences of opinion.

6. Bloodhounds are the best choice for use in a search because they have 60 times the tracking power of German shepherds, can discriminate among scents, and can follow your child's scent in the air as well as on the ground—which means that they may be able to follow your child's scent even if he or she was carried in someone's arms or in a vehicle.

7. Established groups—rather than individual volunteers—should be recruited for the search because they can gather together a large cadre of people very quickly, they have an inner chain of command that makes communication and training easier, and they have an internal screening mechanism that will help ensure volunteers' soundness of character.

8. The volunteer staging area should be located away from your home to protect your family from the accompanying traffic and chaos.

9. All volunteer searchers reporting for duty should be required to show their driver's licenses and to list in a log book their names, addresses, and organizational affiliations. If possible, law enforcement should run background checks on volunteers to guard against the involvement of misguided individuals.

Key Points (continued)

10. Not all parents can or will want to be actively involved in the long-term search for a child. If you want to stay involved, develop a plan and set up a timetable with goals for continuing the search for your child, and set up a schedule of regular visits with your investigator to review the status of your child's case.

11. Keep the public aware of your plight by publicizing any new information about your child—such as a sighting or an interesting lead. Also, if your child has been missing for several years, ask NCMEC to develop an age-progressed picture, then place this picture next to the original picture on shirts, buttons, and posters.

12. Reread your notebook or journal periodically in case you find a passage that triggers a new idea or reminds you of something you had previously forgotten.

13. Consider hiring a private detective only if you are convinced that he or she can do something better than what is being done by law enforcement. Always ask for and check references to find out if the investigator is legitimate, make sure the detective has experience working with law enforcement, insist that all expenses be itemized, and report to law enforcement any offers to bring your child back immediately for a specific sum of money.

14. Be extremely cautious before you allow a psychic to become involved in your child's case. Give all psychic leads to law enforcement for thorough investigation.

Checklist: Gathering Evidence in the First 48 Hours

One of the most critical aspects in the search for a missing child is the gathering of evidence that may hold clues about a child's disappearance or whereabouts. The mishandling of evidence can adversely affect an investigation. Similarly, the collection and preservation of evidence are key to finding a missing child. Parents play a vital role in finding a missing child by providing critical information to law enforcement, by protecting evidence in and around the home, and by gathering information about persons or situations that might hold clues. The following are some tips on what you should do to help law enforcement conduct a thorough and complete investigation.

☐ **Secure your child's room.** Even though your child may have disappeared from outside the home, your child's room should be searched thoroughly by law enforcement for clues and evidence. Don't clean the child's room, wash your child's clothes, or pick up your house. Don't allow well-meaning family members or friends to disturb anything. Even a trash bin or a computer may contain clues that lead to the recovery of the child.

☐ **Do not touch or remove anything from your child's room or from your home that might have your child's fingerprints, DNA, or scent on it.** This includes your child's hairbrush, bed linens, worn clothing, pencil with bite marks, diary, or address book. With a good set of fingerprints or a sample of DNA from hair, law enforcement may be able to tell whether your child has been in a particular car or house. With good scent material, tracking dogs may be able to find your child.

☐ **Do not allow anyone else to sleep in your child's bed, play with his or her toys or computer, or use his or her bedroom for any purpose.** Law enforcement dispatch should advise you not to disturb any part of the house until a thorough search of the scene has been conducted. Investigators should let you know when their search is complete.

☐ **Be prepared to give investigators all the facts and circumstances related to the disappearance of your child.** This includes knowing where your child was last seen, where your child normally went to play, what your child was wearing, and what personal possessions your child had with him or her.

☐ **Describe in detail the clothing your child was wearing and any personal items in the child's possession at the time of the disappearance.** Specify color, brand, and size. If possible, have someone obtain replicas of clothing, hats, purses, backpacks, or other items your child had or wore at the time of the disappearance. Give these articles to law enforcement for them to release to the media and to show to searchers. Make sure you mark these items as duplicates or replicas.

☐ **Make a list of personal identification marks and specific personality traits.** Describe birthmarks, scars, tattoos, missing teeth, eyeglasses, contacts, speech patterns, and behavioral traits. If possible, find photographs that show these unique features. If you have fingerprints of your child or a DNA blood sample, also give these to law enforcement.

☐ **Gather together personal items, such as baby teeth, old baseball caps, or old toothbrushes.** These items may contain hair or blood samples that may be useful as DNA evidence. Also look for pencils or toys that contain impressions of your child's teeth.

☐ **Think about your child's behavior and routine.** Be prepared to discuss where your child played or hung out, what was the usual route taken to and from school, and what other paths of travel might have been taken. Be specific about what your child did for recreation, including playing outdoors, surfing the Internet, and other activities.

☐ **Try to remember any changes in your child's routine or any new experiences.** Look at personal and family calendars to see if they contain clues as to your child's whereabouts or the identity of the abductor. For example, during the past year, did your child join a soccer team, change teams, or get a new coach? Did your child start playing or hanging out in a different area? Did your child keep a diary that might hold clues?

☐ **Try to remember if your child mentioned any new friends.** Talk with your child's friends and teachers to see if they know of any new friends or other contacts your child recently made.

☐ **Find recent photographs of your child in both color and black and white, then have someone make multiple copies of the photographs and keep the originals in a safe place.** Check your cameras for undeveloped film because the most recent photos of your child may be found there. Ask family members and friends to do the same. Give law enforcement multiple photos showing different poses. Steer away from formal or posed photos that do not look like your child. Being careful not to damage the photo, mark the back of each picture with your child's name, address, date of birth, and age when the picture was taken.

☐ **Find videotapes or movies of your child and make copies.** Also ask family members and friends if they have videotapes or movies of your child, perhaps at birthday parties, soccer games, and so forth. Give law enforcement copies that show your child's expressions and mannerisms.

☐ **Make a list of family members, friends, acquaintances, coaches, teachers, and other school staff.** Write down as many telephone numbers and addresses as you can. Offer information for prior in-laws and relatives as well. Include on your list anyone you feel might have something against you or your family.

☐ **Make a list of everyone who routinely comes to your home.** Your list should include postal workers, meter readers, garbage collectors, repair persons, salespeople, pizza delivery persons, and so forth.

☐ **Make a list of new, different, or unusual people or circumstances in and around your home or school within the past year.** Think about if you or any of your neighbors had any home remodeling or house repairs done within the past year. Were any houses listed for sale in your neighborhood in the past year? Has there been any road construction or building in the area? Have any traveling carnivals passed through the area?

☐ **Ask your child's doctor and dentist for copies of the child's medical and dental records and x rays.** Give copies of all medical and dental records to law enforcement for use in the investigation.

Notes

CHAPTER 2

Law Enforcement

To give your child the best chance of being found, you and law enforcement must treat one another as partners.

—Don Ryce

Few parents have had experience working with law enforcement agencies. Perhaps you have had contact previously with law enforcement as a result of a traffic ticket or an accident. If so, you probably saw law enforcement as the enforcer of rules that had been broken—not as a lifeline.

But when your child is missing, you and law enforcement become partners pursuing a common goal—finding your lost or abducted child. As partners, you need to establish a relationship that is based on mutual respect, trust, and honesty. As partners, however, you do not have to agree on every detail. This chapter provides insight into the relationship you are entering into with law enforcement—what you can expect from the investigation, what types of questions you are likely to be asked, and what situations you and your family are likely to encounter in the process.

Your Partnership With Law Enforcement

Most people do not believe that they will be victims of crime—or that their children will be victimized. But if a young member of your family becomes a victim, you will likely wonder what law enforcement expects of you and what you can expect of law enforcement. Understanding these expectations will deepen your knowledge of law enforcement's role, establish a sound basis for your

When asked if it bothered me to take a lie detector test, I told the reporter, "They can electrocute me if it will bring my son back."

—Claudine Ryce

relationship with the agencies and organizations that are there to help, and assist you in handling this all-too-sudden change in circumstances.

Make sure law enforcement understands that your child is in danger and that his or her absence is likely to be involuntary. If your child is 10 years old or younger, it will not be hard to show that your child is in danger. However, if your child is older than 10, it is important to let law enforcement know that your child's absence is not normal behavior and that you would be surprised if your child had disappeared voluntarily.

Ask your law enforcement agency if it uses the AMBER Alert Plan (America's Missing: Broadcast Emergency Response). The AMBER Alert Plan is a voluntary partnership between law enforcement agencies and broadcasters to activate an urgent bulletin in the most serious child abduction cases (see page 4 for more information on the AMBER Alert Plan).

Check to see if any money, clothing (other than what your child was wearing), or other personal items are missing. If nothing else is missing, be sure law enforcement is aware of this.

Let law enforcement know how your child is doing in school and if your child has quarreled recently with you or a friend. If you can establish that there is nothing to indicate that your child ran away, it will expedite law enforcement's classification of your child as abducted or endangered.

Be honest, complete, and forthcoming in your statements and answers to law enforcement. Fully disclose all recent activities of and conversations with your child. What may seem insignificant to you may be important to an investigator.

Be prepared for hard, repetitious questions from investigators. As difficult as it may be, try not to respond in a hostile manner to questions that seem personal or offensive. The fact is that investigators must ask difficult and sensitive questions if they are to do their jobs effectively.

Don't feel guilty about relaying suspicions concerning someone you know. It is not often that a total stranger takes a child. You may not want to believe that it is someone that you know, but keep an open mind and consider all the possibilities. Above all else, trust your feelings, instincts, and gut reactions and share them with law enforcement so they can be checked out.

Do everything possible to get you and your family removed from the suspect list. As painful as it may be, accept the fact that a large number of children are harmed by members of their own families, and therefore you and your family will be considered suspects until you are cleared. To help law enforcement move on to other suspects, volunteer early to take a polygraph test. Insist that both parents be tested at the same time by different interviewers, or one after another. This will help to deflect media speculation that one of you was involved in the disappearance.

Insist that everyone close to your child be interviewed. Encourage everyone—including family members, friends, neighbors, teachers, and coaches—to cooperate in the investigatory process. Although polygraph testing is voluntary, refusal to take a polygraph can cause law enforcement to spend time trying

to eliminate an individual from the suspect list through other means and, as a result, take valuable time away from finding the real suspect.

Leave the interviewing of your other children to law enforcement. Do not question your children yourself. Especially with younger children, insist that a law enforcement officer who is trained to interview children conduct the questioning. Many law enforcement agencies have a child abuse unit with officers who are specially trained to work with children.

You can also ask to have a child advocate sit in on the interview with your child. Child advocates are specially trained volunteers who provide assistance and support to children involved in the legal process. Child advocates are normally housed in the district attorney's office, the court, or the law enforcement agency. Ask law enforcement for information about your local child advocate office. If your child is very young, you may be asked to sit in on the interview. Don't be alarmed, however, if law enforcement prefers to interview your children alone.

Be prepared for constant law enforcement presence in your home. For the protection of you and your family, an officer may be assigned to your home on a 24-hour basis. Although this presence may feel intrusive, welcome the officer, and recognize that this person is there to answer calls and take leads, protect you and other members of your family from potential harm, and provide support. If your law enforcement agency is small, however, it may not have the resources to place an officer in your home 24 hours a day. In those circumstances, it is still reasonable for you to ask for added law enforcement protection in your home.

Talk regularly with your primary law enforcement contact. The officer who responded initially to your call for help may not be your permanent family contact. If there is a good chance that your child has run away, for example, your primary law enforcement contact may work in the missing persons unit. If it is suspected that force was used to abduct your child, your case may be handled by a detective from homicide. Find out who your primary law enforcement contact is and get his or her phone and beeper numbers. Make sure that you find out the name of the backup person to call when your primary law enforcement contact is not available.

Pick a time of day for your contact to call you with information. But realize that there will be days when your investigator has nothing to report. Also, designate one person to serve as the primary law enforcement contact for the family. If your investigator is bombarded with telephone calls from family members and friends, valuable time will be taken away from the investigation.

Make sure investigators know that you expect to hear about significant developments in the case from them, not from the media. The flip side of this is that you must honor law enforcement's request not to disclose some pieces of information to the media. Understand, however, that law enforcement may not be able to tell you everything about the case because full disclosure might jeopardize the investigation.

It's okay if you can't tell me anything—just don't lie to me.
—Pat Sessions

Satisfy yourself that law enforcement is handling your child's case properly. All of the agencies involved in the investigation should be cooperating with one another in pursuit of one goal—finding your missing child and getting the predator off the street. The checklist Working With Law Enforcement lists the most important steps that law enforcement can take to find your missing child. The more you understand the investigatory process, the better able you will be to ask questions about it.

However, you should be aware that most law enforcement officers do not have firsthand experience working on a missing child case. If your primary contact cannot answer a question, find out who can. Also, if you feel that your child's disappearance has been classified inappropriately, ask to speak to the officer's supervisor or to someone else who may have more experience in these types of cases. Don't take no for an answer if you feel strongly that something else needs to be done.

Finally, learn about the services that are available from NCMEC, from your state missing children's clearinghouse, and from the television show *America's Most Wanted*. See the Additional Resources section at the end of this *Guide* for addresses, phone numbers, and brief descriptions of some of the services that are available to you.

Key Points

1. You and law enforcement are partners in pursuit of a common goal—finding your lost or abducted child—and as partners, you need to establish a relationship that is based on mutual respect, trust, and honesty.

2. Most law enforcement officers do not have firsthand experience working on child abduction cases, so if you feel that your child's disappearance has been classified inappropriately, speak to the officer's supervisor.

3. In the beginning of the investigation, be prepared for extensive law enforcement presence in your home.

4. Keep the telephone and beeper numbers of your primary law enforcement contact in a convenient location, and choose a time of day for that person to call you with information, realizing that there will be days when your investigator has nothing to report. Designate one person in your family to talk to your contact so investigators can devote their time to the actual search.

5. Law enforcement may not be able to tell you everything about your case because full disclosure could jeopardize the investigation.

6. Be prepared for difficult, personal, repeated questions from investigators. Answer each question as honestly and completely as you can.

7. Do not question your children yourself. Especially with younger children, insist that a law enforcement officer who is trained in interviewing children conduct the interview.

8. Volunteer early to take a polygraph test, and ask that both parents be tested at the same time by different interviewers, or one after another.

9. Because an abductor is often known by the family, insist that anyone close to the child be interviewed. Share any suspicions with law enforcement so they can be checked out.

10. Satisfy yourself that law enforcement is handling your case properly.

Checklist: Working With Law Enforcement

The following checklist describes the most important steps that law enforcement can take as the investigation begins. Use this information to deepen your understanding of the investigatory process. Discuss these steps with your assigned law enforcement investigator, keeping in mind that the order of the steps is likely to vary, depending upon individual circumstances.

- [ ] A BOLO (Be On the Look Out) bulletin can be broadcast to local law enforcement agencies to alert them to your missing child, and a teletype can be sent locally or regionally.

- [ ] Ask your law enforcement agency if it uses the AMBER Alert Plan (America's Missing: Broadcast Emergency Response). Through AMBER Alert, law enforcement agencies and broadcasters activate an urgent bulletin in the most serious child abduction cases (see page 4 for more information on the AMBER Alert Plan).

- [ ] Your law enforcement agency is required by federal law to immediately enter your child's name into the National Crime Information Center (NCIC) registry of missing persons. There is no waiting period for entry into NCIC. If your law enforcement agency has any questions about compliance with this requirement, contact NCMEC.

- [ ] NCMEC may be asked to broadcast fax your child's picture to law enforcement agencies throughout the country. Assistance from Project ALERT (America's Law Enforcement Retiree Team) investigators and Team Adam may be requested. Patterned after the National Transportation Safety Board's system for sending specialists to the site of serious transportation incidents, Team Adam sends trained, retired law enforcement officers to the site of child abductions involving potential harm to the child and involves these officers in cases of child sexual exploitation. These "rapid-response" specialists, who work in full cooperation with federal, state, and local law enforcement agencies, advise and assist local investigators, provide access to NCMEC's extensive resources, and assist the victim's family and the media, as appropriate.

- [ ] Your local FBI Field Office may be notified in case additional services and support are needed.

- [ ] Your state missing children's clearinghouse will be notified and additional services may be requested.

- [ ] The crime scene—the location outside your home where your child might have been abducted—and your child's bedroom will be secured. The officers who respond initially to your call will evaluate the contents and appearance of your child's bedroom and will secure your child's used bedding, clothing, and shoes and place them in clean bags to be used as scent articles. Your child's toothbrush, hairbrush, and other items that might contain DNA evidence will be stored in a safe place, and footprints in dust, mud, or snow will be protected to preserve the scent. You may be asked if personal items are missing, and the last persons known to have seen your child will be interviewed.

- [ ] Tracking or trailing dogs or a helicopter equipped with an infrared or a heat-sensitive device (to detect heat emitted from the body) may be requested after your residence, yard, and surrounding areas have been searched unsuccessfully.

- [ ] Airlines, airports, bus and taxicab companies, subways, ferries, and ports may be advised of the disappearance and given posters of your missing child.

- [ ] Investigators may revisit various "hot spots" or checkpoints either at the same time of day or the same day of the week following the disappearance to see if they can find anyone who has seen something or who recalls something unusual at the time your child disappeared.

- [ ] Your neighborhood watch should be contacted to see if anything suspicious was noticed.

- [ ] The daily log of parking and traffic tickets and traffic stops will be checked to see if anything relates to your child's disappearance.

- ☐ The convicted sex offender registry will be checked to find out if a potential suspect was in the area.

- ☐ Local newspapers should be collected and reviewed to provide possible clues or leads for the search. Local or regional events and activities—such as carnivals, county fairs, festivals, sports events, and music concerts—and want ads for hired help may produce names or clues regarding either the predator or a witness to the disappearance.

- ☐ A procedure for handling extortion attempts should be established.

- ☐ Neighboring jurisdictions should be contacted to find out if incidents of a similar nature have occurred there also.

Notes

The Media

One shot on the evening news is worth 20,000 posters.
—Patrick Sessions

The media can be important allies in the search for your missing child. But media interest in your case may be either intense or lukewarm, depending on the circumstances surrounding the disappearance of your child and the media's judgment of what is newsworthy.

If you are subjected to intensive media coverage, welcome the attention, even though it may feel uncomfortable, because it is the fastest and most important way to distribute information about and pictures of your child. If you find yourself feeling overwhelmed by the amount of attention, ask law enforcement to help you deal with the sudden barrage of reporters and requests for interviews. However, if the media do not take an interest in your case, there are a number of things you can do to get the media involved. This chapter offers suggestions for generating, maintaining, and managing media involvement.

Media Involvement: The First 48 Hours

During the first 48 hours, you need to do as much as you can to generate media interest in the search for your child. The following tips can help.

Contact the media immediately. Media publicity is the best way to generate leads from the public concerning your child. In most cases, the media should be contacted immediately because time is not on your child's side. You can ask law enforcement to make the initial calls to media outlets, but if this is not done within the first hour, call and give the information to the assignment editors yourself. Intense, early media coverage ensures that people will be looking for your child. Sometimes the coverage is so intense it causes an abductor to let the child go.

Ask radio and television stations to run short clips about the disappearance or to break into their regular programming with information, as is done with a weather warning or other emergency broadcast. Don't wait until the evening news to have information disseminated about your child. Time is of the essence.

Although television coverage is crucial in getting out pictures and stories of your child, don't ignore other types of media. Print and radio media reach tens of thousands of homes each day, and they may be more generous in their treatment of your story. Many people are likely to hear about your child's disappearance first on their car radios. Supplement those broadcasts with stories and pictures of your child in the earliest possible edition of your local newspaper.

Law enforcement may need to be convinced that the media are important allies in a missing child case. Sometimes law enforcement is reluctant to get the media involved in an active criminal investigation. If your law enforcement agency is reluctant, you will have to work closely with your primary contact. Point out that swift use of the media has led to the successful recovery of more

> *The media are your best friends. Use them, don't let them use you.*
> *—Claudine Ryce*

than one missing child and that your child's safety and recovery are more important than building a case against a suspect. Emphasize that you are going to be around for interrogation as weeks pass, but your child's life is in imminent jeopardy. Ask if certain information should not be released because it might jeopardize the case or the safety of your child and honor that request. As a last resort, ask NCMEC, your state missing children's clearinghouse, and missing children's organizations to assist in the event that your law enforcement agency does not want to involve the media.

Prepare a media package and give it to all representatives of the media. The media package should include basic information about your child, including:

- A complete description of your child and of the clothing he or she was wearing at the time of the disappearance.

- A description of the place where your child was last seen.

- Black-and-white and color photos.

- A phone number for people to call with possible leads.

- Details of the reward, if one is being offered.

- Other pertinent information that could help in the recovery of your child, such as a suspicious vehicle near the location where your child was last seen.

A media package will ensure that all reporters start with the same information and will reduce the amount of time you spend answering basic questions. When you prepare a media package, make enough copies to distribute, then keep the original in a safe place in case you need it again in the future.

Select someone to function as a media spokesperson if you feel you are not able to speak alone. Audiences identify with the fear and anguish parents feel when their child is missing. Seeing your face and hearing your

Setting Ground Rules

In the very beginning, media interest is likely to be both intense and intimidating. Therefore, it's important for you to establish ground rules as to where and how often you or your spokesperson will meet with the media. The following tips can help.

- Schedule specific times and locations so reporters know when and where they will be able to ask questions and obtain information. Remember that you control the situation—the media do not control you.

- Choose a location that is convenient for you but that allows the media the space they need to cover the story. For example, you may feel most comfortable holding interviews either outside your house or inside one room. That way, you can allow the media to glimpse your child's personal life without letting them become too invasive.

- Don't open up your home to the media without restrictions or limitations. If you do, you will lose all privacy, and the presence of reporters could interfere with officers working at the scene.

- Don't feel that you are personally obligated to provide all interviews or to participate in all media events. Ask law enforcement, your family spokesperson, and other family members to help.

- Remember that you have the ability to set limits in terms of timing, scheduling, and making rules concerning the use of pictures of your other children. Be sure that the media are aware of your rules and that you expect them to be followed.

voice will motivate viewers to look closer at the picture of your child and to search harder for him or her. Therefore, it is best if you can speak on your child's behalf. However, don't feel you need to be a great speaker. Just talk from your heart and let people know you love your child and need their help in finding and bringing your child home. Bolster your confidence by having someone you know stand beside you to provide support and step in if necessary. On the other hand, if you or your spouse feel unable to deal with the media, choose someone you trust to speak for you, and try to stand beside your spokesperson during the interview. The checklist Conducting Interviews With the Media gives more specific tips on interviews with both print and broadcast journalists.

Schedule press conferences and interviews around media deadlines.
The media operate on deadlines. If you schedule a press conference either too early or too late in the day, reporters will find it difficult to finish their pieces in time to meet their daily deadlines. Consult with reporters to find out when and how often they would like to meet with you. Many parents have found 10 a.m. and 1 p.m. to be good times because they give reporters enough time to prepare stories for both the noon and evening news and because many reporters have openings in their schedule at these times.

Do not schedule draining interviews or speeches back to back. Realize that you have limited mental and physical resources and that if you are not fresh, you will not be effective. If you have an opportunity to appear on a popular radio or television show or on a national network, give this engagement priority over others. However, remember that local television and radio stations will be in your community after the networks leave, so work

Stay calm, collected, and focused. Prepare your thoughts and ideas before you get into an interview.
—Don Ryce

to develop a long-term relationship with them. Sometimes you can ask local stations to rerun portions of an interview you did with the national affiliate.

Avoid scheduling press conferences that conflict with an important event. If you want to make an important announcement, such as a reward offer, make sure you aren't competing with another scheduled event. Find out what events are listed in the day book—often kept by Associated Press—which is used by local media to keep track of newsworthy occurrences. Set your press conference for a time when nothing else significant is happening.

Ask NCMEC or law enforcement to contact *America's Most Wanted* on your behalf. The staff of this television program, which broadcasts nationally, have a special interest in helping to recover abducted children.

Be aware of your public status. Although this is not the kind of fame you want, you may attain some sort of "celebrity" standing because of your continuous involvement with the media. This sudden public status can be very intrusive. People will recognize and approach you wherever you go. The media may turn up at any time and any place, asking for information. You may be filmed any time you are in a public place—and even through the windows of your own home, if the photographer uses a powerful lens. Therefore, for your child's sake, conduct yourself as if all eyes were upon you. Realize that you no longer have the same privacy you once had. Try not to be paranoid, but be careful. Don't do things that might cast you in a negative light, but don't feel guilty if you go out to dinner or to the movies to relieve the stress as the days and weeks pass.

Review all media stories, comments, and tapes. Parents, family members, and friends should review all media spots and events in case they contain clues or pieces of information that could help you at a later date. For example, comments by particular individuals, multiple appearances by one individual, or knowledge of personal or confidential information not previously revealed may help to pinpoint either the perpetrator or persons close to the perpetrator.

If your child is returned, don't let him or her review any tapes of the suspect. This may jeopardize identification of the suspect by your child when a lineup is scheduled by law enforcement.

Media Involvement: After the First 48 Hours

At first, you may feel overwhelmed by the intense media interest generated by your child's disappearance. After a week or so, however, if your child has not been found, you may run into the opposite problem. If media interest dies down, you will have to work to keep the story going. Here are some things you can do to keep your child's story in the public eye.

Devise "media hooks" to keep your child's story in front of the public. Schedule a press conference on an important day, such as National Missing Children's Day (May 25), or prepare a press release to coincide with federal or state legislation relating to missing, exploited, or victimized children. Remember, you don't know how long you will have to search for your child, so you need to plan for the long term. Ask a family member or friend to help if you find the task too difficult.

Give the story a new slant. To give the story a new look, you may want to change the tone of your interviews. Try bringing in someone new to discuss the case, such as a politician, sports personality, popular entertainer, or someone close to the investigation.

Pace yourself. Parcel out new developments in the case in separate announcements to spread coverage over a longer period of time. Ask law enforcement to notify the press of significant developments, such as important leads or items found during the physical search.

Keep the story alive by tying it to a variety of events and activities. You can hold a candlelight vigil, announce a reward, or show how celebrations such as a birthday, holiday, or graduation are different without your child. You can tie your child's story to something that will be broadcast repeatedly, such as a popular song on the radio. Then, every time the song plays, it will be a reminder that your child is still missing. If you can create a way for the media to present your child's story in a different way, it is more likely to be run. Remember that media attention increases when you hold special events and when anniversaries come up. Also, remember to coordinate all events and activities with law enforcement because they can be an important part of the overall investigative strategy.

> **O**nce a reporter made some incredibly insensitive comments about our missing child in front of his siblings. We resolved their hurt and anger by talking the situation over in a family meeting and deciding how to deal with such questions in the future.
> —Patty Wetterling

Victim's Bill of Rights

Appearing on air, whether television or radio, is a new experience for most people. The anxiety produced by this new experience, combined with the trauma of the initial victimization and the retelling of it, underscores the need for parent victims to maintain control over the situation. The following guidelines were written by the National Center for Victims of Crime to minimize the possibility of a second victimization inflicted by the mishandling of a story by the media.

- You have the right to say no to an interview.

- You have the right to select the spokesperson or advocate of your choice.

- You have the right to select the time and location for media interviews.

- You have the right to request a specific reporter.

- You have the right to refuse an interview with a specific reporter even though you have granted interviews to other reporters.

- You have the right to say no to an interview even though you have previously granted interviews.

- You have the right to release a written statement through a spokesperson in lieu of an interview.

- You have the right to exclude children from interviews.

- You have the right to refrain from answering any questions that make you uncomfortable or that seem inappropriate.

- You have the right to know in advance what direction the story about your victimization is going to take.

- You have the right to ask for review of your quotations in a storyline prior to publication.

- You have the right to avoid a press conference atmosphere and to speak to only one reporter at a time.

- You have the right to demand a retraction when inaccurate information is reported.

- You have the right to ask that offensive photographs or visuals be omitted from airing or publication.

- You have the right to conduct a television interview using a silhouette or a newspaper interview without having your photograph taken.

- You have the right to completely give your side of the story related to your victimization.

- You have the right to refrain from answering reporters' questions during trial.

- You have the right to file a formal complaint against a reporter.

- You have the right to grieve in privacy.

- You have the right to suggest training for the media on how they can prevent additional traumatization for victims.

- You have the right to be treated with dignity and respect by the media at all times.

Reprinted with permission from the National Center for Victims of Crime, 2000 M Street NW., Suite 480, Washington, DC 20036, www.ncvc.org.

Develop rapport with someone in radio, television, and print. If a reporter or editor takes a special interest in your story, that person can help you devise ways to get your child's story back in the spotlight. Keep a list of names, telephone and fax numbers, and personal and professional interests. Although reporters often change stations, newspapers, and cities, remember that they can take a story with them wherever they go.

Identify the assignment editors for each news organization, and send your press releases to their attention. Assignment editors are the ones who decide which events to cover and whom to assign as reporters. If you plan an event, let the news organization know what is happening by faxing a news release. Give the facts of the case, along with a news "slant."

Consider granting exclusive interviews. In the beginning, you probably will not want to grant an exclusive interview because interest will be high and you will want the broadest coverage possible. Also, granting an exclusive interview to one news organization over another may offend the one that you leave out. Later, however, an exclusive interview may be appropriate, such as to one station that has developed a story independently or to a national media group such as ABC, CBS, CNN, FOX, or NBC. In some cases, an exclusive interview may be the only way to get a particular aspect of your story out.

Use the media to appeal for special help. The media can be a very effective tool in asking for help. If you need volunteers, training, printing, or equipment that is prohibitively expensive or not readily available, ask the media to broadcast your request. Give a wish list to local radio stations because they in particular are often willing to publicize such appeals as a public service or interest report. Not only can this provide you with the help you need, but it can be yet another hook to remind the public to keep looking for your child.

If possible, obtain the help of a media expert. Sometimes professionals working in the field of public relations donate their services to parents. Because these professionals are very savvy in their dealings with the media, they can be a tremendous help.

Public Awareness Events

Media attention generates leads and keeps your story in front of the public. The following ideas are also excellent ways to involve volunteers in the search campaign.

- Appear on radio and television programs to discuss your child's disappearance.

- Hold a press conference or other media event on your child's birthday or on the anniversary of the disappearance.

- Prepare press releases or make personal statements about the disappearance of a child in another community.

- Prepare press releases relating to federal, state, or local legislation.

- Publish a letter to your child in your local newspaper.

- Ask radio stations throughout your state to play your child's favorite song and dedicate it to your child.

- Hold a rally at your child's school with music and prayers.

- Ask your child's school to organize a letter writing campaign to politicians, the media, or your state legislature.

- Organize student marches to distribute fliers or posters.

- Develop buttons or T-shirts with your child's picture and a special message to your child.

- Hold a prayer vigil.

- Hold a candlelight vigil.

- Organize a dance or a benefit auction.

- Give a special award to the law enforcement officer who served as your primary law enforcement contact.

- Ask sports teams in your area to include pictures of your child in their programs and to make public service announcements at all games.

- Plant a tree or dedicate a garden in your child's name.

- Release helium-filled balloons with your child's name and other relevant information printed on them.

- Hold bowling tournaments.

- Hold running, dance, or other types of marathons.

- Ask local businesses or banks to dedicate a Christmas tree or a display of lights in honor of your child.

Key Points

1. The media should be contacted immediately after your child's disappearance—either by you or by law enforcement—because media publicity is the best way to generate leads from the public. Time is of the essence.

2. If your law enforcement agency is reluctant to involve the media in an active criminal investigation, work closely with your primary contact to convince the agency that media attention has led to the successful recovery of more than one missing child.

3. Prepare a package to give to all representatives of the media that includes a complete description of your child and of the clothing he or she was wearing at the time of the disappearance, a description of the place where your child was last seen, a phone number for people to call with leads, details of the reward (if one is being offered), and black-and-white and color photos.

4. Your pleas for help will be most effective if you personally speak to the media on your child's behalf, but if you cannot do that, ask someone you trust to stand beside you and step in if necessary or to be your spokesperson.

5. Schedule interviews and press conferences around media deadlines, and consult the Associated Press day book to help you avoid scheduling press conferences that conflict with an important news event.

6. Devise "media hooks," such as candlelight vigils or birthday celebrations, to keep your child's story in front of the public. Parcel out new developments in the case in separate announcements to spread coverage over a longer period of time.

7. The media, especially local radio stations, can be an effective tool in asking for help.

8. Be aware that you have become a public person and that the media may turn up at any time and any place to ask questions or to capture your activities on film. Although being in the spotlight might feel intrusive, such attention means that people are interested in learning more about your case.

9. If you suspect that your child has been abducted, ask NCMEC or law enforcement to contact *America's Most Wanted* on your behalf.

10. If your child is returned, don't jeopardize identification of the perpetrator by allowing your child to review tapes of the suspect.

Checklist: Conducting Interviews With the Media

The most successful media interviews happen because of advance planning. If you know beforehand what points you want to get across, you are more likely to have a positive experience with the media. The following tips can help.

☐ **Articulate the most crucial information in every interview.** Before you set up an interview, be sure you are ready. Be prepared to discuss information pertinent to the case—but be sure that law enforcement has been consulted about what information can be released and what should remain confidential. Give essential information consistently to everyone in the media, especially the following items:

- Pictures of your child, in both black and white and color, if possible.

- A description of the clothing your child was wearing and of the items your child had in his or her possession, such as a book bag, backpack, or bicycle, along with identifying characteristics and personal traits.

- A telephone number for people to call in leads.

☐ **Ask that your child's picture be included in every interview you grant.** This is crucial because often the only thing that is clearly known is what your child looks like. Make sure that the picture given to the media resembles your child and is suitable for distribution. Always hold up a picture of your child during an interview and insist that his or her face be shown as part of the story. Ask radio stations to include a description of your child as part of their story.

☐ **Limit the number of points you want to make and keep them simple.** Organize your thoughts and ideas, perhaps by writing them down, before you speak to an interviewer. Stay as calm and focused as you can. Remember that you will be given a very small amount of air time. That means that the more you say, the less control you will have over what portion of an interview the media will play.

☐ **Try to cover the most important points first and to contain your answers to 10- to 20-second "sound bites."** Short answers are more likely to be used than long, drawn-out answers. Also, if you try to cover too much, you may find that your most important points are left out of the story.

☐ **Make your child real by sharing stories that show his or her wit, interests, and other endearing qualities.** If you personalize your plea by showing favorite toys, telling short anecdotes, and airing representative videotapes of your child, people are more apt to listen and remember and to feel they have a reason to care about your plight. However, don't loan any original items to the media because you may not get them back. Always label your child's pictures, videos, and possessions.

☐ **Keep control of the story.** Be prepared to field difficult questions. Although many reporters have families and will empathize with you, their job is to give the public an interesting story. Some may appear to be skeptical of you—at least initially—because of well-publicized disappearances in which the parents turned out to be the culprits.

☐ **Regardless of the questions asked, keep the story focused on your missing child.** If a reporter digs a skeleton out of your closet, don't be afraid to say that a previous event has nothing to do with the present disappearance. You may need to point out that members of the same family can be totally different in terms of behavior, academic performance, and emotional maturity.

☐ **Be patient with reporters because many of them may be young and inexperienced.** It is difficult for someone who is not yet a parent to imagine what you are going through. If you are asked an inappropriate question, don't answer it—and don't explain why.

☐ **Do not lie to the media.** If you are caught in a lie, reporters will never trust you again. But remember that you don't have to answer every question. The only reason you are giving an interview is to find your child. You don't have any obligation to help the media carry a story in a direction you don't want it to go. If you believe a question is insensitive or irrelevant, either say so and decline to answer or else give the information you want to present regardless of the question that was asked. Take control of the situation. Make the points you have to make and insist on getting your message across.

☐ **Do not disclose information to the media that your law enforcement contact has told you to keep confidential.** Consult with your law enforcement agency in advance to find out what information can be released and what information should remain private. Remember that there is no "off the record" comment. If reporters want confidential information, they will try to get it. Consider holding joint press conferences with law enforcement as a way to keep information flowing to the media yet protect confidential details.

☐ **Never publicly criticize law enforcement.** Sometimes reporters ask questions intended to create controversy over law enforcement's handling of a case. Resist the temptation to criticize law enforcement, however, even if you are unhappy with something that has been done. You want the story to be about your child, not about a controversy with law enforcement. You also don't want to risk alienating the people who are spearheading the effort to find your child. Instead, channel any complaints you have through the appropriate law enforcement person or office.

Notes

CHAPTER 4

Photo and Flier Distribution

The more people who know that your child is in danger and what your child looks like, the better the chances are that someone will recognize your child and report his or her whereabouts.

—Claudine Ryce

Distributing pictures of and information about your missing child is an essential part of the search and recovery process. During the first 48 hours, it is critical that recent pictures of your child and facts pertinent to the disappearance be given to law enforcement, the news media, and nonprofit organizations and agencies. Physical traits and personality characteristics should also be described as specifically as possible. This chapter contains important tips about photo and flier distribution and can guide you through both the short- and long-term process.

Photo and Flier Distribution: The First 48 Hours

Search for the most recent pictures. Don't look for pictures in your scrapbook. See if your camera has undeveloped film in it and, if so, take it to be developed. Ask family members and friends if they have recent pictures or videos of your child from a birthday party, holiday celebration, sports event, or school outing. Almost always, your child's school will have a copy of the latest school picture or will be able to tell you the name and telephone number of the school photographer. Even a passport picture, school identification card, or driver's license is better than nothing.

Pick out pictures that most resemble your child. Remember that posters and fliers will show only the head, neck, and top of the shoulders. Candid shots are fine, as long as the facial image is clear. Several pictures from different angles may give people a better idea of what your child looks like. When selecting

photos, keep the purpose in mind—to enable people to recognize your child, not admire a poster that flatters but does not look like your child. For examples of fliers, a sample template, and other items that can be distributed, see the collage on pages 38–39.

Videos or home movies are excellent choices for airing on television. Videos capture your child's appearance, mannerisms, and voice quality. They offer the added advantage of engaging the hearts of viewers, who can relate to the image on the screen as a live personality. Such viewers are more likely to be on the lookout for your child or even to volunteer to help in the search effort.

Ask someone to have copies made of the pictures and videos you select. Photographs can be duplicated quickly by Eckerd Drug Store, K-Mart, Kinko's, PIP Printing, and most camera supply shops. Some businesses may give you a discount rate if you give them your child's case number showing that you have reported your child as missing to the police.

Put all photo originals and negatives in a safe place. Never give away your only copy of a picture, unless you don't care if you get it back.

If the picture was taken by a professional photographer, you may need to get permission to have the picture reproduced. Under most circumstances, professional photographers will be glad to help by giving permission to reproduce a picture once you explain your situation. Some may even reproduce the pictures for you free of charge, so don't be afraid to ask. At the same time, if possible, have the pictures digitized onto a

NONFAMILY ABDUCTION SAMPLE

NAME OF CHILD

CHILD'S PHOTO

CHILD'S PHOTO

DIFFERENT ANGLE

(Date of Photo)

(Date of Photo)

Date Missing: Age Now:
Missing From:
Birth: Age Disap:
Sex: Race:
Height: Weight:
Hair: Eyes:

ID Info:

Circum:

ANYONE HAVING INFORMATION SHOULD CONTACT
The National Center for Missing & Exploited Children®
1–800–843–5678

OR

LOCAL POLICE DEPARTMENT INFORMATION

Note: A missing child must be registered with the National Center for Missing & Exploited Children®
before adding the organization's name and telephone number to this flier.

Source: National Center for Missing & Exploited Children®.

Nonfamily Abduction

MORGAN NICK

Age Progressed

UNKNOWN SUSPECT

DOB: sep-12-1988
Missing: jun-09-1995
Age Now: 13 years
Sex: F Height: 4'0" - 122 cm
Weight: 55 lbs - 25 kg
Hair: Blonde
Eyes: Blue
Missing From:
ALMA
AR
USA

Abductor
DOB:
Sex: M
Hair: Salt & Pepper
Eyes: Unknown
Height: 6'0" - 183 cm
Weight: 180 lbs - 82 kg

Morgan's photo is shown aged to 12 years. She was abducted by an unknown white male while she was playing at a ballpark in Alma. The composite sketch portrays someone who may have come in contact with Morgan at the ballpark. His height and weight are approximations, and he is believed to have been between the ages of 23 and 38 at the time of the abduction. Morgan has five visible silver caps on her molars. She was last seen wearing a green Girl Scout shirt, blue denim shorts and white tennis shoes.

NATIONAL CENTER FOR
MISSING & EXPLOITED
CHILDREN

Family Abduction

GUADALUPE AGUIRRE

Age Progressed

ROSA VENTURA

DOB: feb-05-1989
Missing: apr-06-1992
Age Now: 13 years
Sex: F Height: 3'0" - 91 cm
Weight: 32 lbs - 15 kg
Hair: Black
Eyes: Brown
Missing From:
FRESNO
CA
USA

Abductor
DOB: may-17-1970
Sex: F
Hair: Black
Eyes: Brown
Height: 5'0" - 152 cm
Weight: 125 lbs - 57 kg

Guadalupe's
Flight to A
her face. Gu

NATIONAL CENTER FOR
MISSING & EXPLOITED
CHILDREN

Endangered Runaway

BRIAN ANDREWIN

Age Progressed

DOB: aug-25-1978
Missing: jul-10-1995
Age Now: 24 years
Sex: M
Hair: Black
Eyes: Brown
Height: 5'8" - 173 cm
Weight: 135 lbs - 61 kg
Missing From:
CHICAGO
IL
USA

Brian's photo is shown aged to 19 years. Brian was last seen playing basketball with some friends in a local park on July 10, 1995. He hasn't been seen or heard from since. He has a birthmark on the right side of his neck and a small scar on his eyebrow.

NATIONAL CENTER FOR
MISSING & EXPLOITED
CHILDREN

ANYONE HAVING INFORMATION SHOULD CONTACT
National Center for Missing & Exploited Children
1-800-843-5678 (1-800-THE-LOST)
Chicago Police Department (Illinois) - Youth Headquarters - 1-312-745-6052

floppy disk that can be used to send the picture by e-mail to nonprofit organizations across the country that have access to the Internet.

Put someone persuasive in charge of photo distribution. Ask your photo distribution coordinator to keep a log showing who was given a picture or videotape, then to follow up to make sure that the photographs were distributed. In addition to local media outlets, local civic and business groups, and volunteer groups, copies of your child's photograph can be sent to local government agencies. Permission can be obtained from county commissioners, agency officers, or whoever has authority to post your child's fliers in buses, at bus and subway stops, in tollbooths, at rest stops, and in federal and state parks and buildings.[1]

Get as many individuals and organizations as possible to distribute your child's picture. Start with your neighbors and friends. Then call NCMEC, your state missing children's clearinghouse, and private, nonprofit missing children's organizations in your state and surrounding states, eventually blanketing the country. Ask them to distribute your child's picture through their networks and to display it on their Internet site. Make use of today's high-speed communication links to distribute your child's picture throughout the country.

> *Private businesses throughout our state donated large color reward posters, labels showing our son's face, a toll-free number for people to call if they had seen our son, mailing envelopes, and more than $9,000 in postage so we could send 25 reward posters to every U.S. Congressperson and every state Governor, with a special plea asking them to put up posters of our son in a heavily trafficked area of their home communities.*
> —Claudine Ryce

If you are not hooked up to the Internet, contact someone who is. The Internet allows you to transmit clearer pictures of your child more quickly and less expensively than you could by fax. First, you must have your child's picture scanned and digitized—that is, put on a computer disk. A print or computer shop can provide this service to you. Next, call individual organizations to obtain their e-mail addresses. Now, you can use your disk to simultaneously send your child's picture by e-mail to a wide variety of organizations. The alternative is to purchase separate color pictures and then send your child's picture to each organization via overnight mail, which is a far slower and more expensive process than digitizing and sending them via e-mail.

Ask your photo distribution coordinator to find out where your child's picture has been posted. Check the Internet sites of NCMEC, your state missing children's clearinghouse, and private missing children's organizations to find out where your child's picture has been distributed. Expand the area of distribution to cover the entire country during the second 24-hour period by including the U.S. Customs Service, Border Patrol, and Coast Guard.

Plug into NCMEC's photo distribution services. NCMEC posts photos of missing children on its Web site (www.missingkids.com). On average, 12,190 visits are made on the site

---

[1] By Executive memorandum, NCMEC distributes fliers of missing children to federal agencies for posting in their buildings.

each day, and many companies and agencies have links to this site. In addition, NCMEC can coordinate national media exposure through its partnership with major newspapers, magazines, television networks, and corporations.

Ask your primary law enforcement contact to request that NCMEC send a broadcast fax to its network of law enforcement agencies. NCMEC has the capability to broadcast fax posters and other case-related information to more than 26,000 law enforcement agencies, FBI Field Offices, state missing children's clearinghouses, the Border Patrol, and medical examiners' offices throughout the country. NCMEC can send your child's picture to its network of agencies as soon as your law enforcement agency or the investigating agency makes a request. NCMEC case management personnel are available oncall to make emergency posters, broadcast faxes, and distribute photographic images in the evenings and on weekends.

If your child has been abducted and is in danger, ask law enforcement or NCMEC to contact *America's Most Wanted* on your behalf. You need to ask either NCMEC or your law enforcement agency to make this call. *America's Most Wanted* can be reached by calling 800–CRIMETV (800–274–6388). The program can run a missing children alert, which is a public service announcement showing your child's picture.

Photo and Flier Distribution: After the First 48 Hours

After the first 48 hours, draw on your imagination and the ideas of your many contacts to keep your child's picture and story alive before the public. Here are some ideas of what can be done.

Be creative and aggressive in getting your child's posters put up in heavily trafficked areas across the country. Get approval for your mail carrier to place fliers in mailboxes. Ask utility companies to distribute fliers as their meter readers make their routes. Ask churches to request that their members include your child's flier in Christmas cards and other letters. Ask banks and other groups that make regular mailings to include copies of your child's flier. Ask Federal Express, United Parcel Service, local pizza companies, and other delivery companies to distribute fliers on their routes. Ask trucking lines or moving companies to post pictures on the backs of their trucks. Ask airline pilot and flight attendant unions to request that members post fliers in cities where airline personnel lay over. Call motorcycle clubs and other groups that hold national meetings to see if their members will take along fliers for distribution. If anyone helping you has difficulty convincing a company to post or distribute your child's picture, you personally should get on the phone because it is harder to say no to a victim parent. The checklist Distributing Fliers contains further tips for flier production and distribution.

Prepare a press kit for distribution to national news and talk shows and magazines. Ask local public relations firms or persons with writing ability to help you prepare the kit and to secure e-mail and street addresses. Be sure to include local and regional radio stations. Your law enforcement agency can also give you guidance on press kit preparation.

Look for events where volunteers can distribute fliers. Have volunteers research and make a list of events such as sports contests, county fairs, festivals, and concerts planned in your community, state, and region. Distribute fliers to those events as part of your overall canvassing plan.

Send press releases and arrange interviews during special or seasonal events. Consider celebrating your missing child's birthday by reading aloud cards or special messages you hope he or she will hear. Speak at what would have been your child's graduation from elementary or middle school. Distribute age-progressed photos of your child and updated case information to refresh people's memories and renew interest in your child's plight. Enlist the aid of celebrities and politicians who can help publicize your child's case.

Continue to work with NCMEC and its photo distribution program. More than 400 private-sector participants use NCMEC's print photographs, and a number of federal agencies place NCMEC photos in their mail as well. ADVO, a direct-mail company, disseminates NCMEC's photographs of missing children to up to 85 million homes each week, with pictures of more than 80 different children issued each year. About one in six children who have been featured in the ADVO photo distribution program have been recovered. NCMEC electronically distributes approximately 70,000 posters of missing children monthly to all Wal-Mart stores and Sam's Clubs across the country. In addition, the U.S. Postal Service has a photo distribution program in place that sends fliers by fax to post offices nationwide for display and for dissemination by mail carriers.

Make your own picture cards to insert in mass mailings. Get permission from government agencies, utility companies, and private businesses to have your card inserted in newspapers and envelopes containing state license renewals, tax assessments, local utility bills, payroll envelopes, and bank statements. Talk to direct-mail advertising companies to gain access to mass coupon mailings.

Ask national groups for help. Ask law enforcement associations, women's auxiliary groups, civic groups such as the Rotary Club or Elks and Moose lodges, the Chamber of Commerce, military groups or associations such as the Veterans of Foreign Wars, and college fraternities to distribute and post your child's poster or flier.

Ask a variety of franchise businesses to distribute posters through their normal supply lines. Consider especially various fast food and gasoline chains. Individuals who

A Word About Fax Machines

If you do not own a fax machine, look for one you can rent or borrow, or get permission to use the fax number of a nearby business or police station. You can use it for quick and inexpensive communications with:

- Law enforcement.
- The news media.
- Missing child agencies.
- State missing children's clearinghouses.
- Other individuals and organizations that are willing to help.

When a face-to-face meeting cannot take place—or if information needs to be disseminated quickly—a fax machine can provide you with an important link to your law enforcement agency as you work together to prepare and review press releases, set up interview schedules, or provide lists of the names and telephone numbers of individuals who may hold clues to the whereabouts of your child. A fax machine in your home will also enable you to call organizations devoted to missing child issues, ask them to fax their intake forms to you, and then fill out, sign, and fax back the forms immediately.

know who has abducted or who is holding your child may frequent liquor stores and adult bookstores more often than banks, post offices, and schools. Reward posters should be posted where people with information are most likely to see them.

Consider using publicity gimmicks to etch your child's face in the public's memory. Have your child's picture printed on buttons, T-shirts, bumper stickers, stamps, and baseball-type cards.

Appear on talk shows on the condition that your child's picture is shown during the program. Be sure that the subject of the talk show is compatible with the seriousness of your child's situation and that the show's topics and other guests can be verified prior to your appearance. Make sure that the storyline will help, not harm, you and your child. Steer clear of sensational shows that focus on serial child murders, child sexual exploitation, or other issues that can take the focus away from your case.

Key Points

1. During the first 48 hours, it is critical that recent pictures of your child, descriptions of physical traits and personality characteristics, and facts pertinent to the disappearance be given to law enforcement, the news media, and nonprofit organizations and agencies.

2. Distribute only recent pictures that resemble your child. Remember that posters and fliers will show only the head, neck, and top of the shoulders.

3. Choose representative videos or home movies for airing on television to show viewers your child's appearance, mannerisms, and voice quality.

4. Never give away your only copy of a picture or video.

5. Be both creative and aggressive in getting your child's posters put up in heavily trafficked areas across the country.

6. Use publicity gimmicks, such as buttons, T-shirts, and bumper stickers, to etch your child's face in the public's memory.

7. Prepare a press kit for distribution to national news and talk shows and magazines.

8. Extend your search to the Internet, which will allow you to send your child's picture to a wide variety of organizations via e-mail more quickly and less expensively than you could by fax.

9. Plug into available photo distribution services, including NCMEC, which can coordinate national media exposure, send a broadcast fax to its national network of law enforcement agencies, contact *America's Most Wanted* requesting that a public service announcement be aired on your behalf, and post photos of your child on its Web site.

10. If your child has been missing for a long time, distribute age-progressed photos and updated case information to refresh people's memories and renew interest in your child's plight.

Checklist: Distributing Fliers

Effective fliers creatively combine photographs with basic information about your child. The following checklist can help you develop strategies for increasing the visibility of your child's case and generating possible leads about the disappearance.

☐ **Ask someone creative to take charge of flier and poster production.** Friends, family members, and volunteers can help with this task. Your poster coordinator can ask local printers to produce fliers free or at a discount rate. You can also work through NCMEC, whose case managers are authorized to contact your local PIP Printing store and make arrangements for several hundred copies of fliers to be printed at no charge to the parent. Special requests for larger quantities have been granted for children who are in particular danger.

☐ **Have fliers printed in different sizes for different purposes.** Use different sizes for buttons, handouts, reward posters, mailings, and labels. Use the samples in this chapter as a guide.

☐ **Ask your primary law enforcement contact what telephone number should be published on the flier for people to use to call in tips.** Because the purpose of fliers is to generate leads and tips relevant to your child's case, it is crucial to include a special phone number for readers to call. Often, law enforcement prefers to use a 24-hour hotline staffed by trained information takers rather than the local police telephone number, which may revert to voice mail or a beeper when no one is in the office. The NCMEC toll-free number can be used only after your child has been reported missing to NCMEC. Crime Stoppers and other reputable hotlines experienced in taking lead information are other possibilities. If you ask, Crime Stoppers may be willing to give and take reward information. **Do not use your own telephone number or establish your own 800 number. You need to keep your own phone line free for your child or the person holding your child to call.**

Notes

CHAPTER 5

Volunteers

The many offers of support you receive in the first few days will carry you through. When people ask what they can do, try to tell them something specific. Tomorrow they may be gone, and you are likely to forget who made the offer.

—Pat Sessions

One of the most heartwarming things you will experience is a tremendous outpouring of caring from family members, friends, and strangers. People of all races, nationalities, religions, and socioeconomic levels will offer you and your family emotional support, food and other gifts, and help in the search. In fact, volunteers are essential to the search process. They can and will play a variety of roles in the effort to find your child. This chapter offers suggestions for ways to involve volunteers in the search and ideas for managing offers to help.

Making the Best Use of Volunteers

To make the best use of volunteers, select a volunteer coordinator who is organized, efficient, and able to work well with and give direction to others. The role of the volunteer coordinator is not to handle volunteer activities directly, but rather to delegate to others management of specific activities, such as bringing food to the family, providing water for the searchers, and coordinating distribution of posters and fliers. Choose someone who is practical, well organized, and skilled in providing leadership.

Keep a running list—or have someone keep a list for you—of the things you need as they arise. If you keep your list current, new volunteers will always have a way to get involved, and returning volunteers will know where to go to find out what is needed next.

When someone offers to help, write down the person's name, telephone number, and type of service preferred. When your child is first missing, it is hard to think of what you need now, much less what you will need in the future. If you have no ready answer for someone who asks to help, write down specific information that will enable you to contact that person later with a particular task.

Don't be afraid to ask for what you need. No task is too small or too large. If you need something, the best thing you can do for yourself is to ask. You will be truly amazed by the amount of support you receive. People really do want to help.

Tap into the network of resources that private clubs, businesses, and agencies have available to them. Many local clubs, businesses, and agencies can help in a variety of ways—by donating items, distributing photographs and fliers, or participating in the search. Make a list of what you need, and see what each group can provide. Here are some of the types of organizations that may be willing to help:

- Rotary clubs and other civic organizations.

- Red Cross chapters.

- Local posts of Veterans of Foreign Wars.

- Local lodges.

- Churches and synagogues.

- Parent-teacher associations.

- Scout troops.

■ Retiree organizations.

■ Labor unions.

■ Military installations.

■ Printers.

■ Paper suppliers.

■ Pizza franchises.

■ Fast food chains.

■ Liquor store chains.

■ Airline companies.

■ Taxicab and bus companies.

■ Trucking companies.

■ Public and private transportation agencies.

■ Hospitals.

■ Colleges and universities.

■ Political groups.

Be aware that some volunteers may want to become too involved, to get too intimate with the family, or to act beyond their designated responsibility. Some individuals seem to enjoy media attention. They try to shift the focus of attention away from your child and onto themselves. Unfortunately, not all volunteers may have your best interests in mind but are there for personal reasons. Sometimes individuals who victimize children are drawn to a search scene. If you feel uncomfortable with anyone or anything for any reason, inform your volunteer coordinator or law enforcement contact. Also, don't use unknown volunteers to do personal tasks, such as washing laundry or helping with carpools. Instead, rely on friends or family members for these jobs.

Suggested Volunteer Activities

Volunteers can do many things for you. Let them. In doing so, you allow people to fulfill their desire to help, and you relieve yourself of the burden of trying to do everything yourself, which you cannot. The following activities are particularly well suited for volunteers.

☐ **Participate in the physical search.**

☐ **Canvas area businesses for donations of supplies needed for the search effort or for the family's upkeep.**

☐ **Design posters or fliers.**

☐ **Tack up pictures and posters and hand out fliers.**

☐ **Contact nonprofit organizations, community groups, or other agencies in the community for donations or other assistance in producing or distributing posters.**

☐ **Keep track of all donated items and write thank-you notes.**

☐ **Answer the home telephone 24 hours a day and maintain a telephone log.**

☐ **Prepare meals.**

☐ **Help with household chores, such as cleaning, doing laundry, watering flowers, mowing the lawn, maintaining the yard, or shoveling the driveway.**

☐ **Run errands, such as shopping for groceries or going to the pharmacy.**

☐ **Take care of pets.**

☐ **Form prayer groups.**

Using Untrained Volunteers in the Search Effort

Typically, law enforcement is the coordinating force behind the search, but volunteers often play a major role, especially in the immediate search of the 3- to 5-mile radius around where your child was last seen.

Designate a volunteer search coordinator to work with law enforcement. The volunteer search coordinator will need instruction from law enforcement to determine:

■ How many nonpolice personnel will be needed in the search.

■ What locations or areas are to be searched and on what schedule.

■ What training will be provided to volunteers.

■ How information will be disseminated among volunteers.

■ What specific instructions will be given to volunteers about the process, procedures, and parameters of the search.

Even though private individuals, organizations, and businesses may be interested in helping with the search, it is usually easier to work with an organized group. Organized groups can quickly mobilize large, cohesive groups of searchers and can work through an already established chain of command that will reduce battles for leadership and control. Groups can choose their own team leaders who can serve as a bridge between the volunteer search coordinator and the volunteer searchers. The volunteer search coordinator's

I was devastated when a year later one of our volunteers was arrested for molesting boys in our community.
—Patty Wetterling

task of conveying information to the volunteer searchers will be easier because the team leader can be asked to explain to each group what needs to be done.

Law enforcement, the volunteer search coordinator, and the team leaders should work together to make sure that volunteers are doing what they are supposed to do. Sometimes, overwrought volunteer searchers go beyond their designated roles and responsibilities and may unwittingly impose themselves on the missing child's family. The checklist Working With Volunteer Searchers summarizes the most important points that need to be covered with volunteers.

Make sure that a list of the names and addresses of all volunteers is kept. You will need this list to write thank-you notes, and law enforcement may need it during the search and investigation.

Using Trained Volunteers in the Search Effort

Project ALERT (America's Law Enforcement Retiree Team) provides law enforcement agencies with free consultations on cases involving missing children. Project ALERT was launched by NCMEC in 1992 to link trained, retired volunteers with law enforcement agencies involved in cases of missing children. The following services are provided:

■ An emergency response team of seasoned investigators who can offer additional personnel, search coordination, and other critical resources.

- Specialized training to law enforcement agencies to help them resolve recent or long-term missing child cases.

- Experienced public speakers who can make effective presentations on child safety issues and prevention strategies.

Law enforcement agencies can request the services of Project ALERT or Team Adam by contacting NCMEC, which will donate all resource materials, make all travel arrangements, and pay for all travel costs.

Many nonprofit organizations located throughout the country are poised to help you find your missing child. Many organizations are devoted to the search for missing children. They can help distribute your child's poster, coordinate volunteer activities, locate the nearest bloodhounds, or find a parent of another missing child to give you advice and support. Contact NCMEC to find out the

No one completely understands your pain, but people genuinely care and want to help you, so try to overlook any behavior or comments that seem insensitive.

—Colleen Nick

names and telephone numbers of organizations that meet their requirements for certification or membership. NCMEC's Family Advocacy Division provides case-specific intervention that enhances the services NCMEC offers to children and their parents. The division proactively works with families, law enforcement, and family advocacy agencies to provide technical assistance, referrals, and crisis intervention services. The division supports Team H.O.P.E., a support network of trained volunteers who have experienced an abduction in their own families. These volunteers are matched with families of missing children to offer advice, assistance, and encouragement. You might also want to talk with your primary law enforcement contact and with other parents of missing children. Be wary of organizations that promise they can find your missing child, that request payment for these services, or that are unknown in this field.

Key Points

1. Volunteers are essential to the search process. They can and will play a variety of roles in the effort to find your child.

2. The role of the volunteer coordinator is not to handle volunteer activities directly, but rather to delegate to others management of specific activities, such as bringing food to the family, providing water for the searchers, and coordinating distribution of posters and fliers.

3. If you need something, the best thing you can do for yourself is to ask for help. You will be amazed by the amount of support you receive from others.

4. Keep a running list—or have someone keep a list for you—of the things you need as they arise.

5. When someone offers to help, write down the person's name, telephone number, and type of service offered so you can contact that individual later when you are prepared to accept the offer.

6. Don't use unknown volunteers to do personal tasks, such as washing laundry or helping with carpools. If you feel uncomfortable with anyone or anything for any reason, inform your volunteer coordinator or primary law enforcement contact.

7. Many local clubs, businesses, and agencies can help in a variety of ways—by donating items, distributing photographs and fliers, or participating in the search. Make a list of what you need, and see what each group can provide.

8. Even though private individuals, organizations, and businesses may be interested in helping with the search effort, it is usually easier to work with organized groups, which can quickly mobilize large, cohesive bands of searchers and can work through an already established chain of command.

9. Make sure that a list of the names and addresses of all volunteers is kept so thank-you notes can be written and law enforcement can refer to it during the investigatory process.

10. Be wary of organizations that promise they can find your missing child, that request payment for these services, or that are unknown in this field.

Checklist: Working With Volunteer Searchers

Before the physical search for your child begins, your law enforcement agency will review important policies and procedures for volunteer searchers. The purpose is to make sure that the search is as thorough and effective as possible, that all clues and pieces of evidence are safeguarded, and that the safety of volunteers is protected. Some of the topics that will be discussed with the volunteer searchers include the following.

☐ **Personal items and other supplies for the search.** Based on time of day, climate, and terrain, searchers will be asked to bring with them—or they may be provided with—items for personal use or for use in the search. These items include water bottles, flashlights, batteries, sunscreen, insect repellent, maps, compasses, walkie-talkies, notebooks, and pens.

☐ **Reporting procedures.** Procedures will be established for searchers to use when they report and sign in. The system may be as simple as signing a name or as elaborate as taking a picture or video.

☐ **Search procedures.** Searchers will be given instructions concerning:

■ What type of search is being conducted.

■ What to do if clues or pieces of evidence are found.

■ What to do if a searcher gets hurt or lost.

■ Who is responsible for searchers in a particular area and what is the chain of command for reporting information.

Notes

CHAPTER 6

Rewards and Donations

A reward for the safe return of your child might be what it takes to persuade someone who knows something to speak up.
—Don Ryce

It's hard to assess the true value of a reward in recovering a missing child. The offer of a reward might renew media interest in reporting on a missing child, or it might be the thing that motivates a person living on the fringe of society to call in a lead. Although rewards do not always produce the right leads or have the anticipated results, the use of a reward may be worth considering. This chapter discusses some important issues for you to think about before setting up a reward. It explains how to manage reward or donation funds correctly and where to go for help or advice.

Monetary Rewards

Regardless of the odds that a reward will work, most parents will want to offer one if they possibly can in an effort to turn over every stone in the search to find their missing child. However, many issues need to be considered before an informed decision about a reward can be made.

Get expert help. Because of the number of legal and technical issues that can arise from a reward offer, you need expert advice from a knowledgeable attorney, your primary law enforcement contact, your banker, and the parents of other missing children who have successfully established a reward fund. Make sure that the people who give you advice have firsthand experience managing a reward fund.

Be aware that your reward offer can become a legally enforceable contract. If you offer a reward, you are agreeing to pay a sum of money if a person's actions lead to the requested result. That means that anyone who complies with the terms of the offer can be legally entitled to claim the reward and can sue for its recovery. That's why you must be very careful in how you describe the terms of the reward offer. Sloppy language can result in serious legal problems. Ask an attorney for pro bono legal assistance.

Be prepared to meet resistance from law enforcement. Some law enforcement agencies disapprove of reward offers because they can result in a torrent of false leads. Keep law enforcement informed of any decision you make regarding a reward, and if you sense concern or resistance, point out that all it takes is one solid lead to recover your child. Also, the desire for reward money could motivate an abductor to keep a child alive.

Clearly state the purpose of the offer. First decide what you want the reward to accomplish, then make sure that this purpose is clearly spelled out in the offer. For example, it is a good idea to make your child's *safe* return a written condition of the reward. The better the description of the reward's purpose, the less likely it is that you will have to argue later over whether someone complied with the terms of the offer.

Set a time limit for the reward. One of the goals of a reward is to generate immediate results in order to get your child back quickly. In the beginning, you may want to keep the time limit fairly short and tie it to a significant event, such as your child's birthday. The drama of such a countdown could generate substantial public interest. Avoid open-ended rewards that can result in liability many years later. You can always renew the reward for a longer period of time.

Be careful in establishing the amount of the reward. Don't offer more money than you can afford to pay. Decide on the maximum amount of the reward in the first offer and stick to it because if you raise the amount later, people may wait for a more lucrative offer before calling in a lead.

Check to see if special reward funds already exist. Sometimes state and local agencies—and even the FBI—have funds available to put up as a reward in cases involving predatory abduction. Ask your law enforcement contact to help you find out about such funds.

Be aware that monetary pledges are not as reliable as donations. It is much easier to persuade people to pledge money toward a reward than it is to get them to donate cash. Therefore, you can in theory raise much more money through pledges than you can through donations. The problem is that you cannot be sure that a pledge will be honored when the time comes to pay out the reward. If you use pledges, get the pledge in writing, pay attention to the expiration date of the pledge, and plan to spend a fair amount of time making sure your pledges are still legitimate. Pledges are not forever.

Do not use your personal funds to finance the reward. As hard as it may be, refrain from using your own personal funds for the reward. Based on the terms and conditions spelled out in the reward offer, you may be liable for payment of the reward, and you may even be sued. And though you may not realize it in the

beginning, you may be faced with financial constraints months or years later, for example, if you are out of work for an extended period of time helping in the search for your child.

Monetary Donations

Monetary donations can be extremely helpful to families whose lives have been turned upside down by the disappearance of a child. They can be used to help finance the search, fund a reward, or support the family if a parent is unable to work during the search process. But donations can also present problems if they are not managed properly. For this reason, you need to be aware of some important accounting and accountability issues that, if not handled correctly, could result in legal and financial ruin.

> *After the search fund for our daughter was established, the rumors began to fly about the new vehicles and houses we had purchased. We even heard about a fabulous vacation we supposedly had taken with the money from the fund.*
>
> —Colleen Nick

Make sure that both you and your contributors know how the money will be used. Donations can be used for many different purposes, depending upon your need. Ask that donations be earmarked for a specific purpose—such as the reward fund, the search fund, or the family support fund—and if they are not, ask one of your volunteers to call the donor to find out to which fund the donation should be given. Seek professional help from both a lawyer and a banker to help you establish separate trusts and accounts and to oversee disbursements.

Keep separate bank accounts for each fund. If accounts are set up properly, donors will feel comfortable that records of the money are being kept and that donations are being used for the specified purpose. Creating a trust fund—or at least establishing safeguards, such as requiring dual signatures on checks and maintaining accurate records—is crucial. You must make sure that funds earmarked for a specific purpose are, in fact, being used for that purpose.

Avoid having direct control over any funds received. Parents should not solicit funds on their own. Use volunteer groups for this purpose instead. Parents also should not have any signatory control over the funds because there have been instances in which someone attempted to extort the reward money from parents by force. Protect yourself from this kind of danger by putting the money, and the power to access it, in someone else's hands.

Designate trusted individuals outside the family to have signature authority over the accounts. By removing yourself from the control of the funds, you eliminate any unnecessary scrutiny by members of the public or the media about the use of the funds. Make sure that the individuals selected for this task are trustworthy and that they understand their role and potential liability.

Maintain accurate records that show where the donations came from and how the money was spent. Make sure that the individuals with signature authority maintain proper records on all income and expenditures. A list of donors should be maintained so thank-you letters can be sent, and copies of receipts for all expenditures should be kept in case questions arise. Ask a banker to help you establish proper accounting procedures, or ask for pro bono help from an attorney or an accountant.

Be honest with the public. Be prepared for questions, which may turn into accusations, concerning the use of donated funds. Designate one person—who could be you or a trusted friend or family member—to answer all questions concerning how the funds are being spent. Information concerning the number of donations or the amount in the accounts should never be released to the media.

Specify what will happen to the reward in the event your child is located before the money is spent. Sometimes large sums of money in a reward fund are left unspent. Therefore, you need to establish written procedures for how the money is to be dispensed if it cannot be used for the reward. For example, you can specify that all donations over a certain amount are to be returned, if the donor is traceable, or that unused funds are to be donated to an organization or agency that helped with the search. Excess reward fund money should never be used for the family's personal expenses because that was not the purpose of the fund. Again, talk with an attorney to determine how to handle this situation.

Key Points

1. Most parents will want to put up a reward in an effort to turn over every stone in the search for their missing child, even though it is not known whether rewards actually help in cases involving a missing or abducted child.

2. Use a reward offer to renew media interest in reporting on a missing child or to motivate a person living on the fringe of society to call in a lead.

3. Be prepared for resistance from your law enforcement contact because of police fears that the reward offer will result in a torrent of false leads.

4. Because of the number of legal and technical issues that can arise from a reward offer, you need to obtain expert advice from a knowledgeable attorney, your law enforcement contact, your banker, and the parents of missing children who have successfully established a reward fund. Make sure that the people who give you advice have firsthand experience managing a reward fund.

5. Your reward offer can become a legally enforceable contract, which means that anyone who complies with the terms of the offer can be legally entitled to claim the reward and can sue for its recovery.

6. Monetary pledges are not as reliable as donations.

7. Don't use personal funds to finance the reward, and don't offer more money than you can raise.

8. Keep separate bank accounts for each type of fund—reward, family support, or search—and maintain accurate records showing where each monetary donation came from and how the money was spent.

9. Avoid having direct control over any funds received by designating trusted individuals outside the family to have signature authority over the accounts. By removing yourself from control of the funds, you eliminate any unnecessary scrutiny by members of the public or the media about the use of the funds.

10. Establish written procedures detailing how the money is to be dispensed if it cannot be used for the reward.

Checklist: Selecting a Tipline for Leads

Selecting a phone number for people to use to call in leads for the reward requires careful thought. Your home and business telephones should be reserved for your personal use. NCMEC operates a toll-free telephone line. However, NCMEC staff are prohibited from supplying information about rewards. Moreover, callers with leads have specific needs that must be addressed.

☐ **Callers must be able to give anonymous tips.** Some people will not call unless they can be assured of anonymity. Some tiplines assign a special number to each caller to ensure that a particular caller gets credit for the tip.

☐ **Callers must be able to call 24 hours a day.** Some people prefer to call after regular business hours. The telephone number you list should allow people to call at any hour of the day or night.

☐ **Callers must be able to phone long distance without having to pay for the call.** Some organizations offer an established toll-free telephone number you can use to gather tips or other information about your child. Crime Stoppers is one such organization that answers calls 24 hours a day, provides anonymity to callers, and has a good working relationship with law enforcement. Contact your local office of Crime Stoppers to learn more about that organization's system. Also, your local law enforcement agency and your state missing children's clearinghouse may be able to provide further guidance.

☐ **The person who answers the phone must be able to handle this type of call.** Answering a telephone tipline requires a special set of skills. People who answer tiplines need to know how to keep callers on the line, what questions to ask, and how to write down important information.

☐ **Tips must be furnished to law enforcement immediately.** Law enforcement is responsible for evaluating and following up on all tips—not parents, family members, or friends. For this reason, all tips and lead information should be passed on immediately to law enforcement, including the circumstances surrounding them—how they were made, who received them, at what time of day, and so forth.

Notes

CHAPTER 7

Personal and Family Considerations

I had no rational thoughts, they were all irrational.

—*Heather Cox*

Hanging on to my sanity for a minute at a time often took all of my energy. I could not begin to look several days down the road.

—*Colleen Nick*

Not knowing where your child is or how he or she is being treated is one of the hardest things you will have to face. One minute you will feel a surge of hope, the next, a depth of despair that will threaten your very sanity. Life will become an emotional roller coaster that won't really stop until you can hold your child in your arms again.

As you enter more deeply into the nightmare, know that you are not alone. Unfortunately, other families have had to travel this path and have experienced the same emotional wringer. Families can and do survive—and yours will, too, but it will take all the strength, hope, and willpower you can muster.

Regaining Your Emotional and Physical Strength

Your ability to be strong and to help in the search for your child requires that you attend to your own physical and emotional needs. Although it may be hard right now for you to maintain your daily routine, it is paramount that you do so. The driving force behind the search effort is you, and therefore you must, for your child's sake, be physically and mentally well in order to handle it. The fact is, the nightmare will continue until your child is found, so you need to take as many breaks from it as you can.

Force yourself to eat and sleep. Your body needs food and sleep in order to endure this ordeal. Although eating and sleeping may seem incredibly difficult, you must try. If eating regular meals feels like too much of a drain or if it brings back painful memories of your child, change your meal times and locations. If you cannot sleep at night because you are nervous, tense, or afraid of nightmares, find a place to relax and nap during the day. Just make sure you are doing everything you can to take care of yourself.

Find time for physical exercise. Any type of physical activity, even walking the dog, can help to ease the stress on your body and clear your head. Physical exercise also can help you relax at night so your body gets the sleep it needs.

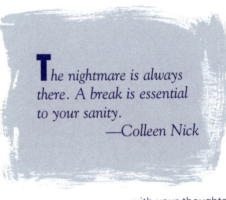

The nightmare is always there. A break is essential to your sanity.
—*Colleen Nick*

Create space for yourself. Find a place of refuge—away from the pressure of the search and the investigation—where you can be alone with your thoughts and regroup. Even a few quiet minutes can significantly relieve stress.

It may help to walk in the park, visit your church or synagogue, or talk to a neighbor. Try to take as much time as you need and can spare. Remember that you are the best judge of what will help you to handle the life crisis and that it is okay—even necessary—to take a break from the stress for dinner and a walk.

Find ways to release your emotions. Your emotions will be running wild and will seem out of control. In these circumstances fear, anger, and grief can take over your entire existence. Therefore, you need to find a way to release your emotions because if you cannot express them, you may find yourself taking it out on others. Talk with someone—a friend, a relative, or a professional therapist—who will just listen. Also, try to stay busy. You can cook, write letters that express your feelings without mailing them, or record your thoughts and feelings in a journal.

My life ended the day my child was taken. At some point I had to find a place to start over.
—Heather Cox

Keep a journal. Some parents find it extremely helpful to keep track of their thoughts and feelings in a journal. Journal entries, which can be written or tape recorded, need not be coherent or intelligent. Their purpose is merely to record your thoughts and feelings at any particular time and to help you resolve them.

Put your anger and grief to work for you. Come up with ideas for the search. For example, you can make a list of all of your child's friends, neighbors, and acquaintances—anyone who might hold a clue as to the whereabouts of your child. You can make a list of places your child frequented or even occasionally visited—anywhere law enforcement could look for your child. Finally, you can think of ways to release your emotions in a productive manner.

Stay away from alcohol and harmful medications. Alcoholic beverages, harmful drugs, and even prescription medications can prevent you from being an effective member of the search team and can even induce depression. However, if you are having trouble sleeping at night or coping during the day, ask your physician for help. He or she may prescribe a medication that will help you sleep or alleviate your depression. Just be sure that you only take medications under the supervision of a physician because some can be addictive.

Don't blame yourself. Looking back, you may feel that there was something you could have done to have prevented your child's disappearance. You can literally drive yourself crazy asking, What if . . . ? But the fact is, if you did not arrange for the disappearance, you should not hold yourself responsible for not knowing or doing something that may seem obvious in hindsight. And remember, children have been abducted out of the safety of their own bedroom while their parents slept in the room next door.

Don't shoulder the blame of others. Recognize that some people may blame you for the disappearance because of their own fears for their children. They may imply that if you had watched your child more closely, he or she would not have disappeared. Blaming you may make them feel somewhat safer in the world because they hold you—and your supposed mistake—responsible for your child's abduction, rather than the abductor. Also, sometimes one spouse blames the other for the disappearance of the child. This is hardly ever fair and can critically harm the well-being of the entire family. Try to stay out of the blame game by being kind to yourself and to one another. Understand that sometimes anger and blame are irrational and misplaced. Keep the lines of communication open among family members. If necessary, seek professional counseling or other outside assistance to help you handle the situation.

Stay united in your fight to find your child. Don't allow the stress of the investigation to drive a wedge into your family life. When emotions run wild, be careful that you do not lash out at or cast blame on others. Instead, give each other lots of warm hugs to counteract the stress inherent in the situation. Remember that everyone deals with crises and grief differently, so don't judge others because they do not respond to the disappearance in the same way you do.

Allow the opinions of other people to be their business, not yours. Some people need to have an opinion as to how well you are handling the situation and whether you should be acting differently. Keep in mind that such judgments are merely the opinions of others and that at any given moment, you are doing the best you possibly can.

Seek peer support for yourself and your family. Some parents find talking with other parents of missing children to be extremely beneficial. Sometimes it is enough to know that you are not alone and that someone else in the world truly understands. Consider contacting one of the parent authors of this *Guide* (listed in the back of this book) or a member of Team H.O.P.E. (see page 77). Call the Child Protection Division at the Office of Juvenile Justice and Delinquency Prevention, U.S. Department of Justice (listed in the Additional Resources section of this *Guide*), to get in touch with any one of the parent authors. You can also ask your law enforcement contact for a list of victim's advocates and local support groups. Nonprofit agencies or your state missing children's clearinghouse can also provide you with the names and phone numbers of parents who can help.

Seek professional counseling for yourself and your family. Professional counseling can be extremely helpful for parents and families to assist them in coping with their feelings of fear, depression, grief, isolation, anger, and despair. You may think that you and your family can or should get through the crisis alone, but you don't have to. Encourage family members to take care of themselves by seeking support and counseling. If you need assistance finding or paying for counseling, contact your local mental health agency or provider or ask another family member or friend to do this for you. If you are uncomfortable with professional counseling, consider another form of support—from your clergy, a physician, a lay counselor, or a friend.

Seek peace and solace for yourself. Many parents find comfort in their faith and use it as a powerful incentive to survive this nightmare. The loneliness of grief diminishes somewhat for people who believe that they are not alone. Turning to—or returning to—religion can give parents the support and encouragement they need at this critical juncture in their lives.

> **M**y daughter Morgan's brother and sister were very young—3 years and 22 months—when she was abducted. Her father and I decided to not let them watch the news on TV, but we kept them informed about the search in a way that they could understand. As a family, we released balloons for her at a set time every month. That let the two children who were left feel like they were helping in the search for their sister.
>
> —Colleen Nick

Mentally Preparing for the Long Term

As heartless as it may seem, your life and the lives of your children must go on. Although moving on with your life may seem impossible, you must do it—for the good of yourself and your family. You will, of course, find that there is no such thing as "normal" life as you once knew it. Everything has changed, and has changed forever. And whatever the outcome, you will be dealing with this nightmare in some way for the rest of your life.

Going back to work is not abandonment of your child. If you need to return to work, you may feel extremely guilty. Try to remember that your child must have a home to return to and that you are working to provide that home for your child. When you return to work, find a quiet place where you can go to be alone or to cry. Your grief is likely to come unannounced, and you will need a place where you can express it. If your job requires a lot of concentration, which you are not able to give, look for another position that does not place as many demands on you. The American Hospice Foundation publication *Grief at Work,* listed in the Recommended Readings section of this *Guide,* has additional advice.

Focus on your emotional well-being. To keep yourself on a more even keel, continue individual and family counseling, and try to stay busy. You can immerse yourself in activities with your other children or volunteer to help in school, church, or the community. Don't isolate yourself. Many parent survivors try to help other parents by working through missing children's organizations or by starting a group of their own. The books and articles listed in the Recommended Readings section of this *Guide* have proven to be particularly helpful.

It's okay to laugh. A laugh can be as cleansing as a good cry. Laughter not only helps to release tension and emotion, it helps to restore normalcy to life.

Never stop looking. You will probably want to dedicate part of each day to your missing child. Use these hours to keep the search going and to keep the hope alive. You can set aside time to make phone calls, write letters, contact law enforcement, or do whatever you think will help in the search for your missing child.

Helping Your Children To Regain Their Physical and Emotional Strength

Your other children need your physical and emotional support now more than ever, but you may not be able to satisfy their needs. You may have barely enough energy to keep yourself going. You may feel that you are abandoning your lost child if you are not doing something every moment to find him or her. These are normal feelings. Consider getting additional support for your other children during this time of crisis. Here are some ideas.

Find a safety zone for your children. Find a safe place away from your home where your other children can be shielded from both the search effort and the media. This is especially important for young children, who still need to play and be themselves. Trusted friends and relatives can provide a reasonably normal, nurturing life for your children in a relatively stress-free environment, so this is a good time to let members of the extended family and friends assume a large part of the responsibility for their care. Just remember to maintain contact with your children—both over the phone and with regular visits—and to reassure them frequently how much you love them.

Consider letting your other children participate in the search. If it seems appropriate, you can allow your older children to actively participate in the search effort. However, it is important to consider their age, desire, and level of maturity and to respect their right to say no. If your children are young, you will need to decide how much information you want revealed and whether it is appropriate for them to participate in the search effort. In some cases, younger children have distributed balloons and fliers. If you decide to let your children participate, keep a gauge on how well they are handling the situation and be prepared to make changes, if necessary. Remember that there are both emotional and security issues to consider when your children participate in the search effort. Ask your law enforcement contact for advice.

Think twice about letting the media interview siblings. Interviews with the media can be extremely traumatic to the brothers and sisters of a missing child. Children are seldom prepared for the extremely personal or probing questions asked by insensitive or pushy media personnel. Remember that the media can and will be persistent, particularly given the sudden ascension of your family to "celebrity" status. Make sure that you supervise interviews and continue to set boundaries that are in your children's best interests.

Bring the needs of your other children into balance with those of your missing child. Focus on the needs of the children who are still at home. Remember that they, too, are trying to cope with their loss. Talk with your children about their feelings of fear, anger, hurt, and loss. Make them feel as important to you as your missing child. Encourage them to return to the interests and activities they enjoyed before the disappearance—by playing with friends, participating in sports, or playing music.

Establish different routines to help your family cope. Family meetings can be an effective way to deal with the changes wrought by the disappearance. They offer family members a safe, nonjudgmental environment in which to voice feelings of fear, anger, and frustration. They also give family members an opportunity to keep one another informed about the ongoing investigation and involved in family decisionmaking.

Celebrate birthdays, holidays, and other special events. Young children will want to celebrate birthdays and holidays even when a brother or sister is missing. Plan ahead so you are not caught offguard by the intense emotional roller coaster that can accompany such events. You can, for example, try changing family holiday traditions and beginning new ones. Instead of throwing a big birthday party, you can eat cake and ice cream for breakfast and then open presents. If you have older children, instead of the traditional Christmas or Hanukkah celebration, you can go on a trip. Remember that your children need to have fun and that they want you to celebrate, even if your heart is not ready for it. Recognize, however, that you have personal limitations as to what you will be able to handle and that those limitations need to be respected. The secret is to plan ahead.

Allow all members of the family to talk about your missing child, about their emotional reactions to the situation, and about their loss. Don't let the absence of your child and your deep sense of loss become a taboo subject. Instead, let your children know that they can freely express their thoughts and feelings to you and that they will be met with love and acceptance. Let your children know that it is okay for everyone in the family—including mom and dad—to cry and that you can help each other by holding hands, giving each other a big hug or kiss, or getting each other a glass of water. Remember that even if you do not communicate with your children about your missing child, other children in the neighborhood will.

> **W**e celebrated Jimmy's life by remembering the profound things he had said and the mischievous things he had done.
> —Claudine Ryce

Don't be surprised if your other children's behavior drastically changes. Everyone in the family has suffered a tremendous shock. In these circumstances, bedwetting, stomachaches, depression, anger, sullenness, quietness, and truancy are common reactions. But by the same token, don't be alarmed if your child's behavior changes very little or not at all. Children, just as adults, react differently to the disappearance of a child.

Help your other children return to some type of normalcy by returning to school. Your children need the normalcy that the daily routine of school provides. But before your children go back to school, talk with them about what they want others to know. Make sure they understand that most people in your community already know what has happened. Listen to your child's thoughts and feelings about returning to school. Then, talk to your child's teachers and counselors to help them prepare for the return of your child.

Ask the school to bring counselors into the classroom both after the disappearance and when your child returns to school. Teachers and classmates of a missing child will also experience fear and grief. When your other children return to school, they and their friends—and the friends of your missing child—are bound to feel scared. Ask your law enforcement contact if an officer can go to the school to teach the children both how to recognize dangerous situations and how to get away. Ask teachers and counselors for their help in giving all of the children the support they need to deal with this crisis. The American Hospice Foundation publication *Grief at School,* listed in the Recommended Readings section of this *Guide,* has additional advice.

Ask other children who have faced similar difficulties to provide one-on-one support to your children. A number of sources can put you in touch with other families that have experienced the trauma of a missing child. Try calling your local law enforcement agency, your state missing children's clearinghouse, NCMEC, or other missing children's organizations. Your children may be more comfortable talking with a peer who has gone through a similar ordeal.

Seek professional counseling for your children. Your children are suffering just as intensely as you are and may need help dealing with feelings of fear, anger, and grief. Don't feel guilty that you cannot be their total support at this point in your life. Instead, look to others to help your children cope with the powerful emotions that follow the disappearance of a brother or sister.

> **W**atching my daughter suffer through the loss of her child was incredibly painful. Not only was I hurting over the loss of Shelby, my granddaughter, but also over the deep pain of my daughter.
>
> —Marion Boburka

Helping Extended Family Members To Regain Their Physical and Emotional Strength

The disappearance of a child affects many people—grandparents, aunts, uncles, cousins. They, too, will experience deep emotional scars from the sudden loss. All of you will need the love and support of one another. Extended family members can do a number of things—contribute to the search effort, take care of other children, or stay in close phone contact—to help them work through the pain and grief of losing a relative.

If possible, include extended family members in the search effort. Extended family members can serve a variety of functions—as spokesperson for the family, coordinator of media events, coordinator of volunteers, or coordinator of searchers. They can also develop and disseminate posters and fliers, contact missing children's organizations to request assistance, and gather information to give to law enforcement to help in the search and recovery effort.

Put a daily report on your answering machine to keep family members informed of progress in the search. Law enforcement should keep you informed about the investigation, but in many cases extended family members are left out of such discussions. They may, as a result, feel left out and unsure of

what to do. Putting simple messages on your answering machine will keep distant family members informed. It also will save you time from having to make or receive phone calls and in the process will help to free up your telephone line in the event that your child or someone with a tip is trying to get through.

Don't try to provide emotional support to everyone in your family. It is not your job to be an emotional "rock" for the extended family. Instead, encourage family members to seek support and comfort from friends and other family members, from their church or synagogue, or from local mental health agencies, professional counselors, or other community resources. Let members of your family know that you are depending on them to help you through this ordeal.

A Word About Starting a Nonprofit Organization

As time passes and your child does not return, you may become very frustrated. You may want to find a way to maintain or increase the level of activity. Some parents think about establishing a nonprofit organization (NPO). An NPO must have a broad public purpose (that is, it cannot be devoted to a single child). Although state regulations vary, federal regulations are in place to assure the public that their contributions are well managed and are used for the organization's stated purpose.

There are several things to consider when establishing a tax-exempt NPO:

- You need a purpose or mission statement, articles of incorporation, bylaws, an operating budget, and a board of directors. You will need to file necessary documentation with appropriate state and federal agencies.

- You must be aware of the differences between for-profit and nonprofit organizations to maintain the NPO's programmatic and fiscal health.

- You need to keep meticulous files, including financial and corporate records. These records are open to the public. You may also have to meet the standards of charitable watchdog agencies.

- You may want to have an existing NPO serve as your fiscal agent.

- You will need to develop a program that attracts enough interest and financial support so it can be maintained.

Key Points

1. Force yourself to eat, sleep, and exercise. Realize that your ability to be strong and to help in the search for your child requires that you attend to your own physical and emotional needs. If you have trouble sleeping at night or coping during the day, ask your physician for help.

2. Stay away from alcohol, drugs, and harmful medications, which can prevent you from being an effective member of the search team and can even induce depression.

3. Find productive ways to release your emotions, such as keeping a journal, talking with a friend, taking a walk, exercising, cooking, cleaning, or thinking up ways to extend the search. Don't isolate yourself.

4. Don't blame yourself for your child's disappearance or allow yourself to shoulder the blame of others. Treat yourself and others as kindly as you can.

5. Don't feel guilty if you need to return to work. Remember that you are working to provide a home for your child to return to.

6. Stay united with your spouse in your fight to find your child. Don't allow the stress of the investigation to drive a wedge into your family life, and don't misjudge others because their response to the disappearance is different from yours.

7. Don't allow the absence of your child and your deep sense of loss to become a taboo subject. Encourage open discussion of feelings in a safe, caring, nonjudgmental environment during family meetings.

8. Establish different routines for daily life and for celebrating birthdays, holidays, and other events. Find a safe place away from your home—perhaps with friends or relatives—where your other children can feel free to play and express themselves, away from the spotlight of the search and the media.

9. If it seems appropriate, allow your other children to participate in the search, perhaps by distributing posters, fliers, or balloons. Remember that both emotional and security issues need to be addressed.

Key Points (continued)

10. Don't be surprised if your other children's behavior changes drastically. Bedwetting, stomachaches, depression, anger, sullenness, quietness, and truancy are common reactions. But remember that children, just like adults, react differently to the disappearance of a child, and some may not show any change in behavior.

11. Help your other children return to some type of normalcy by going back to school, but listen carefully to them before they go. Request that the school bring counselors into the classroom to discuss the situation with the children, and ask your law enforcement contact to arrange for an officer to go to the school to teach the children both how to recognize dangerous situations and how to get away.

12. Extended family members can serve a variety of functions in the search effort—as spokesperson for the family, coordinator of media events, coordinator of volunteers, or coordinator of searchers. They can also help with posters and fliers, request assistance from missing children's organizations, and gather information to give to law enforcement.

13. Don't try to provide emotional support to everyone in your family. Seek professional counseling for yourself and your children to help you cope.

14. Bring callers up to date on the progress of the search by recording simple messages on your home answering machine.

15. Never stop looking. Dedicate part of each day to your missing child by making phone calls, writing letters, contacting law enforcement, or doing whatever you think will help in the search for your missing child.

Checklist: Figuring Out How To Pay Your Bills

Even though your world has stopped, the rest of the world marches on. If you work outside the home, your boss may be understanding at first, but may tell you later that you will be replaced if your child is not found quickly. If you are in business for yourself, you will have to balance your need to participate in the search with your need to make decisions about your company. At some point, you will have to deal with the bills that come in and perhaps other financial concerns as well, even if it's to buy yourself more time.

☐ **Extended leave.** If you need an extended leave from work, ask a family member or friend to talk to your employer on your behalf. For example, some employers allow employees to donate their excess leave time to those who need it.

☐ **Extensions on bills.** Talk to mortgage companies, utility companies, and other creditors to see if you can get extensions on your bills.

☐ **Rebudgeting.** Ask a friend or an accountant to help you rebudget your finances or refinance your house.

☐ **Financial assistance.** Call your state missing children's clearinghouse to find out if they know of local resources, such as social services or emergency or other financial assistance funds, that might be able to provide short- or long-term support for you.

☐ **Victim compensation funds.** Call the Office for Victims of Crime or your state attorney general's office to find out about victim's compensation funds. Such funds may cover lost wages and other crime-related expenses.

Notes

Recommended Readings

Critical Incident Response Group, Child Abduction and Serial Killer Unit. 1997. *Child Abduction Response Plan.* **Quantico, VA: Federal Bureau of Investigation.**

Designed for law enforcement agencies, this document is available only through the Crimes Against Children Coordinator of the local FBI Field Office. It explains essential techniques in child abduction investigations.

Echols, Mike. 1991. *I Know My First Name Is Steven.* **Kearney, MO: Pinnacle Books.**

Though not officially out of print, this book is out of stock indefinitely at the printer. Copies may be available at your local library or in larger bookstores. The author describes the long ordeal of two children who were kidnapped by Kenneth Parnell and the trauma they faced.

Federal Agency Task Force for Missing and Exploited Children. 2004. *Federal Resources on Missing and Exploited Children: A Directory for Law Enforcement and Other Public and Private Agencies.* **Washington, DC: U.S. Department of Justice, Office of Justice Programs, Office of Juvenile Justice and Delinquency Prevention.**

Developed for law enforcement agencies and other federal, state, and local agencies that work with missing and exploited children, this directory describes the many federal services, training programs, and resources that relate to missing and exploited children. Contact information is provided for easy access. The directory is available free of charge by calling the National Criminal Justice Reference Service (NCJRS) at 800–851–3420. If you prefer, you can download copies of the directory from the NCJRS Justice Information Web site (www.ncjrs.org).

Office of Juvenile Justice and Delinquency Prevention. 2002. *A Family Resource Guide on International Parental Kidnapping.* **Washington, DC: U.S. Department of Justice, Office of Justice Programs, Office of Juvenile Justice and Delinquency Prevention.**

This guide was developed by federal, state, and local agencies and organizations, and parents of children abducted to another country by the noncustodial parent. It offers descriptions and realistic assessments of civil and criminal remedies, explains applicable laws, identifies public and private resources, and identifies strategies to help left-behind parents recover their children or reestablish meaningful contact with them in another country. This guide is available free of charge by calling NCJRS at 800–851–3420. If you prefer, you can download copies of the guide from the NCJRS Justice Information Web site (www.ncjrs.org).

Office of Juvenile Justice and Delinquency Prevention. 2002. *A Law Enforcement Guide on International Parental Kidnapping.* **Washington, DC: U.S. Department of Justice, Office of Justice Programs, Office of Juvenile Justice and Delinquency Prevention.**

This guide is a companion to *A Family Resource Guide on International Parental Kidnapping.* It serves as a resource for federal, state, and local law enforcement officers who are called on to respond to international parental kidnapping cases. It offers ideas and suggestions for preventing international abductions; discusses applicable laws, legal remedies, and liability concerns; describes the role of law enforcement as both the initial responder and the investigator; and offers strategies for extradition, reunification, and recovery. This guide is available free of charge by calling NCJRS at 800–851–3420.

Turner, Johanna. 1995. *Grief at Work.* **Washington, DC: American Hospice Foundation.**
This booklet provides suggestions for employees and managers for coping with grief and loss at work. The booklet is available from the American Hospice Foundation, 1130 Connecticut Avenue NW., Suite 700, Washington, DC 20036 (202–223–0204).

Turner, Johanna. 1996. *Grief at School.* **Washington, DC: American Hospice Foundation.**
This booklet for educators and counselors provides suggestions for helping children to cope with crisis and grief in the school setting. The booklet is available from the American Hospice Foundation, 1130 Connecticut Avenue NW., Suite 700, Washington, DC 20036 (202–223–0204).

Walsh, John. 1997. *Tears of Rage.* **New York, NY: Pocket Books.**
This book recounts the powerful and emotional story of John Walsh and his wife Revé following the 1981 abduction and murder of their 6-year-old son Adam. The book also chronicles John Walsh's 16-year exhaustive efforts on behalf of missing and exploited children. Available in bookstores.

Ward, Heather Patricia. 1994. *I Promise I'll Find You.* **Ontario, Canada: Firefly Books.**
This heartwarming children's book tells the story of a mother who promises to do everything humanly possible to find her child should that child ever become lost or missing from home. Available in bookstores.

Publications From the National Center for Missing & Exploited Children®

Single copies of the following books and up to 50 copies of each brochure are available free of charge from the National Center for Missing & Exploited Children® (800–THE–LOST® or 800–843–5678).

Books

Family Abduction Guide

Written in both English and Spanish, this guide describes the actions that parents and family members can take and the laws that can help when their child is abducted.

Missing and Abducted Children: A Law Enforcement Guide to Case Investigation and Program Management

This document provides law enforcement with a step-by-step guide on how to respond to and investigate missing children cases.

Recovery and Reunification of Missing Children: A Team Approach

This report discusses the recovery and reunification of children with their families, with emphasis on a multiagency, multidisciplinary approach.

Brochures

Child Safety on the Information Highway

Teen Safety on the Information Highway

The following brochures, written in both English and Spanish, are part of the Just in Case Series and offer step-by-step instructions for dealing with a variety of issues relating to missing and exploited children.

Just in Case . . . Guidelines in Case You Are Considering Day Care

Just in Case . . . Guidelines in Case You Are Considering Family Separation*

Just in Case . . . Guidelines in Case You Need a Babysitter

Just in Case . . . Guidelines in Case Your Child Is Testifying in Court

Just in Case . . . Guidelines in Case Your Child Might Someday Be a Runaway*

Just in Case . . . Guidelines in Case Your Child Might Someday Be Missing*

Just in Case . . . Guidelines in Case Your Child Might Someday Be the Victim of Sexual Exploitation*

Just in Case . . . Guidelines in Dealing With Grief Following the Loss of a Child

---

* Also available in Vietnamese.

Just in Case . . . Guidelines in Finding Professional Help in Case Your Child Is Missing or the Victim of Sexual Exploitation

Just in Case . . . Guidelines on Using the Federal Parent Locator Service in Cases of Parental Kidnaping and Child Custody

The following brochures, part of the Know the Rules Series, provide information and tips for children, teenagers, and parents on a variety of topics relating to child exploitation, victimization, and safety.

Know the Rules . . . Abduction and Kidnapping Prevention Tips for Parents

Know the Rules . . . After School Safety Tips for Children Who Are Home Alone

Know the Rules . . . Child Safety for Door-to-Door Solicitation

Know the Rules . . . For Child Safety in Amusement or Theme Parks

Know the Rules . . . For Child Safety in Youth Sports

Know the Rules . . . For Going To and From School More Safely

Know the Rules . . . General Parental Tips To Help Keep Your Children Safer

Know the Rules . . . Safety Tips for Halloween

Know the Rules . . . Safety Tips for Teens

Know the Rules . . . Safety Tips for the Holidays

Know the Rules . . . School Safety Tips

Know the Rules . . . Summer Safety Tips for Children

Know the Rules . . . Summer Safety Tips for Parents

Know the Rules . . . When Your Child Is Flying Unaccompanied

Know the Rules . . . When Your Child Is Traveling Unaccompanied by Bus or Train

Knowing My 8 Rules for Safety

Additional Resources

A number of organizations and agencies in both the public and private sector work with parents whose children are missing. These agencies can provide information, assistance with photo and flier production and distribution, referral services, and investigative resources for you, your family, and law enforcement.

Private Resources

National Center for Missing & Exploited Children® (NCMEC)

NCMEC serves a variety of functions:

- Distribution of pictures and posters of missing children worldwide.

- Provision of information and technical assistance to citizens.

- Provision of training, technical assistance, and technical support to state missing children's clearinghouses and to state and local law enforcement agencies.

You can call NCMEC to get copies of its intake and release forms mailed or sent to you via fax and to get information on how you can have a color picture of your child posted on NCMEC's Web site, distributed to NCMEC's photo partners, and printed on fliers for you to distribute.

NCMEC also manages and coordinates Project ALERT (America's Law Enforcement Retiree Team) and Team Adam, free consultation services on missing children cases for law enforcement agencies.

NCMEC's Family Advocacy Division also supports Team H.O.P.E., a parent-to-parent mentoring service. Team H.O.P.E. is a national support network that matches left-behind parents with trained parent volunteer mentors who have experienced an abduction in their own families.

National Center for Missing & Exploited Children®

699 Prince Street
Alexandria, VA 22314–3175
800–THE–LOST® (800–843–5678) (Hotline for the United States, Canada, and Mexico), 800–826–7653 (TTY), or 703–235–3900
703–235–2200 (Fax)
Internet: www.missingkids.com
CyberTipline: www.cybertipline.com

Branch Offices
California: 714–508–0150
Florida: 561–848–1900
Kansas City (MO): 816–756–5422
New York: 585–242–0900
South Carolina: 803–254–2326

Team H.O.P.E.
866–305–HOPE
Internet: www.teamhope.org
or contact NCMEC at 800–843–5678

Association of Missing and Exploited Children's Organizations, Inc. (AMECO)

AMECO is a national association of missing and exploited children's organizations that work together to serve and protect missing children and their families. AMECO seeks to improve both the capabilities of nonprofit missing children's organizations and the overall quality of services provided through certification of its member organizations. AMECO develops standards for missing children's organizations, provides outreach and assistance to local nonprofit organizations, and establishes guidelines for nonprofit agencies that serve missing children and their families.

You can contact AMECO to find out the names of nonprofit missing children's organizations—both in your community and throughout the country—that can provide assistance and support to you and your family.

Association of Missing and Exploited Children's Organizations, Inc.
Internet: www.amecoinc.org

Other Nonprofit Organizations

A number of private nonprofit organizations provide services to families whose children have been abducted. Before you contact such an organization, however, ask NCMEC or AMECO to tell you which organizations meet their requirements for certification or membership. You might also want to talk with your law enforcement contact and with the parents of other missing children. Be wary of organizations that promise they can find your missing child, that request payment for these services, or that are unknown in this field.

Victim's Advocates

Ask your law enforcement contact to arrange to have a victim's advocate come to your home to explain your rights and to explore the counseling, treatment, and related services available to you. Victim's advocates are usually associated with the offices of the sheriff, the state prosecutor, or the district attorney. If you have access to the Internet, you can find a list of victim advocacy and compensation groups at the Office for Victims of Crime Web site (www.ojp.usdoj.gov/ovc). *Federal Resources on Missing and Exploited Children: A Directory for Law Enforcement and Other Public and Private Agencies* (see Recommended Readings) also contains a list of victim's advocate services and organizations.

Parent Survivors

Talking with parents who have survived a similar ordeal can help you regain your sanity and increase your effectiveness in the search for your child, for only they can truly understand your pain and anguish. The parents who helped to write this *Guide* are willing to talk to you. To contact any of the parent authors, call the Child Protection Division at the Office of Juvenile Justice and Delinquency Prevention (202–616–3637). Other victim help groups are listed in *Federal Resources on Missing and Exploited Children: A Directory for Law Enforcement and Other Public and Private Agencies* (see Recommended Readings).

In addition, Team H.O.P.E. can connect trained parent volunteers who can provide advice, assistance, and encouragement to other parent victims. Parent survivors and volunteers can also be reached through Team H.O.P.E. at 866–305–HOPE.

Local Businesses

Local businesses in your community can provide a number of goods and services that will be needed in the search for your child. In addition, with permission you can post your child's picture in store windows, on doors, and on the backs of trucks. See chapter 5 (Volunteers) for a list of the types of organizations and businesses that may be willing to help.

Government Resources

Federal Agencies

Many federal agencies provide technical support and services to law enforcement and other public and private agencies to aid in the search and recovery of a missing child. A comprehensive list of these services is available in *Federal Resources on Missing and Exploited Children: A Directory for Law Enforcement and Other Public and Private Agencies* (see Recommended Readings). The agencies listed below, which have been referenced throughout this *Guide,* provide support and/or investigative services to missing and exploited children and their families.

Child Protection Division

The Child Protection Division provides support to several missing and exploited children's organizations, including NCMEC, AMECO, and Team H.O.P.E.; provides technical assistance and training to law enforcement to improve their investigation of missing and exploited children cases; produces reports to improve services to missing and exploited children and their families; and conducts research related to missing and exploited children. For information about any of these activities or the organizations listed above, call the Child Protection Division at the phone number listed below.

Child Protection Division

Office of Juvenile Justice and Delinquency
   Prevention
Office of Justice Programs
U.S. Department of Justice
810 Seventh Street NW.
Washington, DC 20531
202–616–3637
202–307–2819 (Fax)
Internet: www.ojp.usdoj.gov/ojjdp

Office for Victims of Crime (OVC)

OVC makes awards each year to state crime victim compensation and assistance programs to supplement state funding for victim services. Crime victim compensation is the direct payment to a crime victim or to his or her family to help cover crime-related expenses, such as medical treatment, mental health counseling, lost wages, or funeral services. Every state administers a crime victim compensation program, and most programs have similar eligibility requirements and offer a comparable range of benefits.

Crime victim assistance programs provide direct services, such as crisis intervention, counseling, emergency transportation to court, temporary housing, and criminal justice support and advocacy. For information about these programs, contact your local crime victim compensation program or crime victim assistance program. *Federal Resources on Missing and Exploited Children: A Directory for Law Enforcement and Other Public and Private Agencies* (see Recommended Readings) contains a listing of all state offices.

Office for Victims of Crime

Office of Justice Programs
U.S. Department of Justice
810 Seventh Street NW.
Washington, DC 20531
202–307–5983
202–514–6383 (Fax)
Internet: www.ojp.usdoj.gov/ovc/

Federal Bureau of Investigation

FBI Headquarters

Special Investigations and Initiatives Unit
Crimes Against Children Unit
935 Pennsylvania Avenue NW.
Washington, DC 20535–0001
202–324–3666
202–324–2731 (Fax)
(See the front of your local telephone book for the number of your local FBI Field Office.)

The Crimes Against Children Unit works closely with FBI Field Offices and other FBI components to coordinate operational support to more effectively address crimes against children. The FBI Field Offices house Crimes Against Children Coordinators, who use all available investigative, tactical, forensic, informational, and behavioral science resources in the investigation of crimes against children.

Missing Children's Clearinghouses[1]

Missing children's clearinghouses are state government agencies connected with law enforcement. Because the types of services available in each state vary substantially, you need to call your state clearinghouse to find out both what services are available to help you in your search and whether the clearinghouse will distribute photographs of your missing child. Then you can call other state clearinghouses in your region and throughout the nation to compare services and take advantage of those not available to you in-state. Keep a list of what you learn about each clearinghouse in a spiral notebook for later use.

Alabama

Alabama Bureau of Investigation
Missing and Exploited Children
P.O. Box 1511
Montgomery, AL 36102–1511
800–228–7688
334–353–2563 (Fax)
Internet: www.dps.state.al.us/abi
ORI: ALAST0047

Alaska

Alaska State Troopers
Missing Persons Clearinghouse
5700 East Tudor Road
Anchorage, AK 99507
800–478–9333 or 907–269–5497
907–338–7243 (Fax)
ORI: AKAST0100

Arizona

Arizona Department of Public Safety
Criminal Investigations Research Unit
P.O. Box 6638
Phoenix, AZ 85005
602–223–2158
602–223–2911 (Fax)
ORI: AZ0079925

Arkansas

Arkansas Office of the Attorney General
Missing Children Services Program
323 Center Street, Suite 1100
Little Rock, AR 72201
800–448–3014 (in-state only) or
      501–682–1020
501–682–6704 (Fax)
ORI: AR060035A

California

California Department of Justice
Missing and Unidentified Persons Unit
P.O. Box 903387
Sacramento, CA 94203–3870
800–222–3463 (in-state only) or
      916–227–3290
916–227–3270 (Fax)
Internet: www.caag.state.ca.us/missing/
      index.htm
ORI: CA0349454

Colorado

Colorado Bureau of Investigation
Missing Person/Children Unit
710 Kipling Street, Suite 200
Denver, CO 80215
303–239–4251
303–239–5788 (Fax)
ORI: COCBI0009

---

[1] The ORI numbers following many of the clearinghouses in this list are assigned by the National Crime Information Center to law enforcement agencies for administrative purposes.

Connecticut

Connecticut State Police
Missing Persons
P.O. Box 2794
Middletown, CT 06457–9294
800–367–5678 (in-state only),
    860–685–8190 (emergency messaging),
    or 860–685–8260
860–685–8346 (Fax)
ORI: CTCSP2900

Delaware

Delaware State Police
State Bureau of Identification
1407 North DuPont Highway
Dover, DE 19903
302–739–5883
302–739–5888 (Fax)
ORI: DEDSP0001

District of Columbia

D.C. Metropolitan Police Department
Missing Persons/Youth Division
1700 Rhode Island Avenue NE.
Washington, DC 20018
202–576–6768
202–576–6561 (Fax)
ORI: DCMPD0000

Florida

Florida Department of Law Enforcement
Missing Children Information Clearinghouse
P.O. Box 1489
Tallahassee, FL 32302
888–356–4774 or 850–410–8585
850–410–8599 (Fax)
E-Mail: 74431.134@compuserve.com
Internet: www.fdle.state.fl.us

Georgia

Georgia Bureau of Investigation
Intelligence Unit
P.O. Box 370808
Decatur, GA 30037
800–282–6564 or 404–244–2554
404–244–2798 (Fax)
ORI: GAGBI0050

Hawaii

Hawaii State Clearinghouse on
    Missing Children
Department of the Attorney General
235 South Beretania Street, Suite 206
Honolulu, HI 96813
808–586–1449
808–753–9797 (Hotline)
808–586–1424 (Fax)
Internet: aloha.hgea.org/hsc/index.htm

Idaho

Idaho Bureau of Criminal Identification
Missing Persons Clearinghouse
P.O. Box 700
Meridian, ID 83680–0700
888–777–3922 or 208–884–7154
208–884–7193 (Fax)
Internet: www.isp.state.id.us/identification/
    missing/index.html
ORI: ID001015Y

Illinois

Illinois State Police
500 Iles Park Place, Suite 104
Springfield, IL 62703–2982
800–843–5763 or 217–785–4341
217–785–6793 (Fax)
Internet: www.isp.state.il.us
ORI: IL0849800

Indiana

Indiana State Police
Indiana Missing Children Clearinghouse
Third Floor North
100 North Senate Avenue
Indianapolis, IN 46204–2259
800–831–8953 or 317–232–8310
317–233–3057 (Fax)
Internet: www.in.gov/isp/safetyinfo/mcc/
ORI: INISP0012

Iowa

Missing Person Information Clearinghouse
Division of Criminal Investigations
Wallace State Office Building
East 9th and Grand
Des Moines, IA 50319
800–346–5507 or 515–281–7958
515–242–6297 (Fax)
Internet: www.state.ia.us/missing

Kansas

Kansas Bureau of Investigation
Missing Persons Clearinghouse
1620 SW. Tyler Street
Topeka, KS 66612–1837
800–572–7463 or 785–296–8200
785–296–6781 (Fax)
ORI: KSKBI0000

Kentucky

Kentucky State Police
1240 Airport Road
Frankfort, KY 40601
800–222–5555 (in-state only), 502–227–8799
502–564–4931 (Fax)
Internet: www.kentuckystatepolice.org/
    missing.htm
ORI: KYSKP0022

Louisiana

Louisiana Department of Social Services
Louisiana Clearinghouse for Missing and
    Exploited Children
Office of Community Services
P.O. Box 3318
Baton Rouge, LA 70812
225–342–8631
225–342–9087 (Fax)

Maine

Maine State Police
Missing Children Clearinghouse
State House Station 52
18 Meadow Road
Augusta, ME 04333–0052
207–532–5404
207–532–5455 (Fax)
ORI: MEMSP0000

Maryland

Maryland Center for Missing Children
Maryland State Police Computer Crimes Unit
7155 Columbia Gateway Drive, Suite C
Columbia, MD 21046
800–637–5437 or 410–290–1620
410–290–1831 (Fax)
ORI: MDMSP9500

Massachusetts

Massachusetts State Police
Missing Persons Unit
470 Worchester Road
Framingham, MA 01702
800–622–5999 (in-state only) or
    508–820–2129
508–820–2128 (Fax)
ORI: MAMSP0070

Michigan

Michigan State Police
Prevention Services Unit
714 South Harrison Road
Lansing, MI 48823
517–333–4006
517–336–6100 (24-hour emergency line)
517–333–4115 (Fax)

Minnesota

Minnesota State Clearinghouse
Bureau of Criminal Apprehension
1430 Maryland Avenue
St. Paul, MN 55106
651–793–1107
651–793–1101 (Fax)

Mississippi

Mississippi Highway Patrol
3891 Highway 486 West
Jackson, MS 39208
601–933–2657
601–933–2677 (Fax)

Missouri

Missouri State Highway Patrol
Division of Drug and Crime Control
P.O. Box 568
Jefferson City, MO 65102
800–877–3452 or 573–526–6178
573–526–5577 (Fax)
ORI: MOMHP0014
ORI: MOMHP0007

Montana

Montana Department of Justice
Missing/Unidentified Persons
P.O. Box 201402
303 North Roberts Street, Room 374
Helena, MT 59620–1417
406–444–2800
406–444–4453 (Fax)
ORI: MT025045Y

Nebraska

Nebraska State Patrol
Criminal Records and Identification Division
P.O. Box 94907
Lincoln, NE 68509
402–471–4545/479–4918
402–479–4054 (Fax)

Nevada

Nevada Office of the Attorney General
Nevada Missing Children Clearinghouse
555 East Washington Avenue, Suite 3900
Las Vegas, NV 89101–6208
800–992–0900 (in-state only) or
    702–486–3539
702–486–3768 (Fax)
Internet: www.ag.state.nv.us/Divisions/
    Fraudunits/MissingKids/miss_kids.htm
ORI: NV018025A

New Hampshire

New Hampshire State Police
Investigative Services Bureau
Major Crimes Unit
91 Airport Road
Concord, NH 03301
800–852–3411 (in-state only) or
    603–271–2663
603–271–2520 (Fax)
ORI: NHNSP0800

New Jersey

New Jersey State Police
Unidentified Persons Unit
P.O. Box 7068
West Trenton, NJ 08628
800–709–7090 or 609–882–2000
609–882–2719 (Fax)
ORI: NJNSP0032

New Mexico

New Mexico Department of Public Safety
ATTN: Law Enforcement Records
P.O. Box 1628
Santa Fe, NM 87504–1628
505–827–9191
505–827–3388 (Fax)

New York

New York Division of Criminal Justice Service
Missing and Exploited Children
4 Tower Place
Albany, NY 12203
800–346–3543 or 518–457–6326
518–457–6965 (Fax)
Internet: http://criminaljustice.state.ny.us/
    missing/index.htm
ORI: NY001025Y

North Carolina

North Carolina Center for Missing Persons
4706 Mail Service Center
Raleigh, NC 27699–4706
800–522–5437 (in-state only) or
    919–733–3914
919–715–1682 (Fax)
ORI: NCNHP0000

North Dakota

North Dakota Bureau of Criminal Investigation
P.O. Box 1054
Bismarck, ND 58502–1052
701–328–5500
701–328–5510 (Fax)
ORI: NDRCD0000

Ohio

Missing Children Clearinghouse
Attorney General's Office
Crime Victims Services Section
65 East State Street, Fifth Floor
Columbus, OH 43215–4231
800–325–5604 or 614–466–5610
614–728–9536 (Fax)
Internet: www.mcc.ag.state.oh.us

Oklahoma

Oklahoma State Bureau of Investigation
Criminal Intelligence Office
6600 North Harvey
Oklahoma City, OK 73136
405–879–2645
405–879–2967 (Fax)
ORI: OKOBI0000

Oregon

Oregon State Police
Missing Children Clearinghouse
400 Public Service Building
Salem, OR 97310
800–282–7155 (in-state only) or
    503–378–3720
503–363–5475 (Fax)
Internet: www.osp.state.or.us
ORI: OROSP0003 OROSP0004

Pennsylvania

Pennsylvania State Police
Bureau of Criminal Investigation
1800 Elmerton Avenue
Harrisburg, PA 17110
717–783–0960
717–705–2306 (Fax)
ORI: PAPSP0012

Rhode Island

Rhode Island State Police
Missing and Exploited Children Unit
311 Danielson Pike
North Scituate, RI 02857
401–444–1125
401–444–1133 (Fax)
ORI: RIRSP0001

South Carolina

South Carolina Law Enforcement Division
Missing Person Information Center
P.O. Box 21398
Columbia, SC 29221–1398
800–322–4453 or 803–737–9000
803–896–7595 (Fax)
ORI: SCLED00M0

South Dakota

South Dakota Attorney General's Office
Division of Criminal Investigation
East Highway 34
c/o 500 East Capitol Avenue
Pierre, SD 57501
605–773–3331
605–773–4629 (Fax)
ORI: SDDCI0000

Tennessee

Tennessee Bureau of Investigation
Criminal Intelligence Unit
901 R.S. Gass Boulevard
Nashville, TN 37206
615–744–4000
615–744–4513 (Fax)
ORI: TNTBI0000

Texas

Texas Department of Public Safety
Special Crimes Services
P.O. Box 4087
Austin, TX 78773–0422
800–346–3243 (in-state only) or
    512–424–5074
512–424–2885 (Fax)
Internet: www.txdps.state.tx.us/mpch
ORI: TXDPS4300

Utah

Utah Department of Public Safety
Bureau of Criminal Identification
P.O. Box 148280
Salt Lake City, UT 84114–8280
888–770–6477 or 801–965–4500
801–965–4749 (Fax)

Vermont

Vermont State Police
103 South Main Street
Waterbury, VT 05671
802–241–5352
802–241–5349 (Fax)

Virginia

Virginia State Police Department
Missing Children's Clearinghouse
P.O. Box 27472
Richmond, VA 23261
800–822–4453 (in-state only) or
    804–674–2026
804–674–2105 (Fax)
ORI: VAVSP0000

Washington

Washington State Patrol
Missing Children Clearinghouse
P.O. Box 2347
Olympia, WA 98507–2347
800–543–5678
360–644–2156 (Fax)
ORI: WAWSP00L1

West Virginia

West Virginia State Police
Missing Children Clearinghouse
725 Jefferson Road
South Charleston, WV 25309–1698
800–352–0927 (in-state only) or
    304–558–1467
304–558–1470 (Fax)

Wisconsin

Wisconsin Department of Justice
Division of Criminal Investigation
P.O. Box 7857
Madison, WI 53701–2718
800–THE–HOPE (800–843–4673)
    (in-state only) or 608–266–1671
608–267–2777 (Fax)
ORI: WI013015Y

Wyoming

Wyoming Office of the Attorney General
Division of Criminal Investigation
316 West 22d
Cheyenne, WY 82002
307–777–7537
307–777–8900 (Fax)
ORI: WY0110400

Canada

Royal Canadian Mounted Police
Missing Children's Registry
P.O. Box 8885
1200 Vanier Parkway
Ottawa, Ontario, CN K1G 3MB
877–318–3576 (toll free in North America)
    or 613–993–1525
613–993–5430 (Fax)
Internet: www.ourmissingchildren.ca
ORI: ON11074

Puerto Rico

Missing Children Program
Centro Estatal Para Niños Desaparecidos y
    Victimas de Abuso
P.O. Box 9023899
Old San Juan, PR 00902–3899
787–729–2523
800–995–NINO (limited calling area)
787–722–0809 (Fax)

About the Parent Authors

Shelby Cox

Heather Cox and Marion Boburka, mother and grandmother, respectively, of Shelby Marie Cox, have been strong proponents for missing and exploited children and their families since 4-year-old Shelby disappeared on November 13, 1995. She was playing on the family porch with her older sister and friends. After a 5-day search, Shelby's battered body was found in a neighbor's shed, killed by an 18-year-old boy who later confessed. "Shelby was a joyous child," Heather writes, "who saw the wonders of this world and embraced every one of them. She saw the magic in the clouds, the wonder of a rainbow, the beauty of a flower in bloom. She was full of spunk and mischievousness and laughter. To say we miss her doesn't even come close to how deep our feelings are. Instead, we fight for the children, for Shelby's peers, so that people will learn, and then Shelby's life and death will not have been in vain."

Colleen Nick, mother of Morgan Chauntel Nick, has been a spokesperson and champion for missing children and their families since Morgan's abduction on June 9, 1995. Six-year-old Morgan was last seen at 10:45 p.m., while playing at a little league ball game in Alma, AR. She was standing near her mother's car where she had stopped to empty sand from her shoes. Witnesses observed a man watching Morgan as she played with other children. The man was described as white, 6 feet tall, 20 to 40 years old, with black or "salt and pepper" hair. Colleen writes, "You are a wonderful friend, a treasured daughter, a loving big sister, a blessing we cannot live without. We feel cheated every day that goes by and we do not see your smile, hear your bubbly laughter, or listen to your thoughts and ideas. We know that the world was deprived of something very precious and unique when you were taken from us. We have never stopped believing that we will find you. We will never give up hope. Always know that you are loved. Most of all, don't ever give up. We will find you. We promise."

Morgan Nick

Jimmy Ryce

Don and Claudine Ryce, parents of Jimmy Ryce, have devoted their lives to getting kids home safe. On September 11, 1995, Jimmy was walking home from the bus stop when he was abducted at gunpoint, sexually molested, and murdered. His parents believe he could have been found if bloodhounds had been available. As cofounders of the Jimmy Ryce Center for Victims of Predatory Abduction, Don and Claudine have worked to establish a network of bloodhounds across the country; coordinated a petition drive that resulted in President Clinton's signing of an Executive memorandum requiring that missing children's pictures be posted in federal buildings and national parks; worked to place missing children's pictures on billboards and in every driver's license renewal packet sent out in Florida; and helped the Dade County School Board implement the Jimmy Ryce Predator Notification Act by sending home with each child pictures of convicted sexual predators living in the county. The Ryces write, "Children are their own last defense against sexual predators. To make children more predator resistant, we are developing a Web site (http://jimmyryce.org) where children can learn how to recognize dangerous situations and how to get away. It takes a lot of imagination and hard work to make our children safer, but we can do it together. Send us your ideas at misujim@netrox.net."

Patrick Sessions, father of Tiffany Sessions, has devoted much of his energy to helping protect other children who may be victimized and providing support and encouragement to their families. Tiffany was last seen on February 9, 1989, at 6 p.m., walking in Gainesville, FL. She was 20 years old and had blonde hair and blue eyes. "It is the hope of the Sessions family," Patrick writes, "that this *Guide* will be of help to families who may find themselves in the difficult position of searching for a loved one. Although the search for Tiffany has not been successful, many other families' prayers have been answered with the return of their loved ones. Literally thousands of people, both friends and strangers, reached out

Tiffany Sessions

to help in the search for Tiffany, and those hard-learned lessons are included in this *Guide*. Our small part in helping prepare this *Guide* is dedicated to all the people who have helped Tiffany and the other children who have needed their help and support. Thanks to those people, we have the strength and determination to continue our search for Tiffany."

Patty Wetterling, mother of Jacob Wetterling, has devoted her life to child safety issues. She is a founding member of the board of directors of the Association of Missing and Exploited Children's Organizations, a cofounder of the Jacob Wetterling Foundation, and a member of the board of directors of the National Center for Missing & Exploited Children®. Her most recent accomplishments include passage of the Jacob Wetterling Crimes Against Children Registration Act, a federal law requiring convicted sex offenders to register their place of residence with local law enforcement after release from prison. On October 22, 1989, Jacob was abducted at gunpoint near the Wetterling home and has not been seen since. Patty writes, "I think about you every day and wonder what you would have become had you not been stolen from us. It's so unfair. If you're not alive, we need to know. Someone has been torturing us for far too long. I still look everywhere I go at faces, and I keep asking everyone else to look, too. Sometimes people who were badly victimized forget who they are. I'm still asking the whole world to help. Don't give up your dreams, Jacob. They can still come true if you hope and don't give up. We're still searching for you and we will never quit until we know who did this, what happened, and where you are. Forever and always, I love you."

Jacob Wetterling

Index